the Love Your Heart

(LowCholesterol) Cookbook

by
CAROLE KRUPPA

SURREY BOOKS
101 East Erie Street
Suite 900
Chicago, Illinois 60611

THE LOVE-YOUR-HEART LOW CHOLESTEROL COOKBOOK is published by Surrey Books, Inc., Suite 900, 101 E. Erie St., Chicago, IL 60611.

This book is manufactured in the United States of America.

First edition. 1 2 3 4 5

Library of Congress Cataloging-in-Publication Data:

Kruppa, Carole.
The love your heart low cholesterol cookbook / Carole Kruppa.
288 p.   cm.
ISBN 0-940625-12-1 : $11.95
1. Low-cholesterol diet—Recipes. I. Title.
RM237.75.K78   1990
641.5′638—dc20   89-21725
                                                                                 CIP

Editorial production: *Bookcrafters, Inc. Chicago*
Cover deisgn and art direction: *Hughes & Co., Chicago*
Illustrations: *Elizabeth Allen*

Single copies may be ordered by sending check or money order for $13.95 (includes postage and handling) per book to Surrey Books at the above address. The Surrey Books catalog is also available from the publisher free of charge.

With love to
my husband,
Harvey Stern,
The Light of My Life

Acknowledgments

I wish to thank my friend and publisher, Susan Schwartz, whose faith in my recipes has inspired me to do my best work. My heartfelt appreciation also goes to Joanie Susic, M.S., R.D., who so ably worked out the nutrition calculations; Gene DeRoin, who skillfully handled the editing and production; and Sally Hughes, who designed the book so beautifully.

Contents

Contents

Foreword

One of the most commonly asked questions in my office is, "What is my cholesterol level?" Recently published epidemiologic studies show that for every 2 percent decrease in an elevated serum cholesterol level, there is a 1 percent decline in risk of heart attack. For example, lowering your elevated cholesterol level by 20 percent could reduce your risk of heart attack by 10 percent.

This data has led to an absolute frenzy (as well there should be) among patients, especially ones with heart disease, to follow their serum cholesterol levels like the stock market. The nuances of HDL-cholesterol (good), LDL-cholesterol (bad), and triglycerides (fats) are no longer foreign to the general public. Not too uncommonly I am asked, "Well, doctor, what is my HDL-cholesterol level? How is my ratio?" before I can even relate their total level.

I really do enjoy caring for patients with hypercholesterolemia because the mainstay of treatment is dietary adjustment. This involves a working partnership and a level of honesty ("You're not cheating on that praline ice cream?" as I wag my finger) that helps to cement the patient-doctor relationship. When an elevated cholesterol value is found, I always place the patient on a low-cholesterol and low-fat diet for three to six months prior to decisions regarding medication. Literature, referral to a certified dietitian, and encouragement are the basis for successful dietary therapy.

Dietary adjustments are not easy. Education and encouragement are good beginnings. To successfully lower your cholesterol, however, aggressive attention to and modification of the basic ingredients of your meals, whether prepared at home or in a restaurant, is the starting point. Cookbooks such as Carole Kruppa's *Love Your Heart Low Cholesterol Cookbook* add immensely to the dietary arsenal of anyone trying to fight off old habits. Good food *can* be low in cholesterol.

Eat and be well.

Anne E. Summers, M.D.
Falls Church, Virginia

Introduction

Cocktail party talk now includes discussions of blood cholesterol levels; the subject has become a prime concern to many Americans because the presence of blood cholesterol has been linked again and again to coronary heart disease, the number one killer in the United States. However, the good news is that a diet low in fats and high in soluble fiber can help reduce low-density lipoproteins (LDL), the "bad cholesterol," in the bloodstream.

Cholesterol is a fat-like substance found in every blood cell, and it is essential to the human body. Dietary cholesterol is found in foods originating from animal sources. Take heed: that delicious steak you had for dinner last night and the breakfast sausage you ate this morning are both items you will need to restrict if you want to lower your blood cholesterol level.

Cholesterol is carried through the bloodstream by low-density lipoproteins (LDL), which are believed to deposit the cholesterol along artery walls, potentially causing coronary heart disease. High-density lipoproteins (HDL), or "good cholesterol," is thought to carry cholesterol away from the cells in the arteries and transport it back to the liver for processing or removal.

The maximum dietary cholesterol intake recommended is 300 milligrams (mg) daily; that is the goal you should work toward. On these pages you will find a variety of recipes that will help you reach—or beat—that goal. And the switch to a more healthful way of eating, and lower cholesterol levels, will possibly result in a healthier heart.

A major premise of this book is that it is possible to adopt a low-cholesterol, low-fat, low-calorie diet and still enjoy eating. The recipes will show you how to do it. Controlling weight is very important, and the recipes are designed to minimize calories, too. The use of herbs and spices is encouraged because with them you can control your intake of sodium (salt), which has been linked to high blood pressure in some people.

This book of recipes has been prepared to help you switch to a low-fat, low-cholesterol diet as enjoyably as possible. We have provided shopping tips, cooking suggestions, and a section on how to adapt your own recipes to your new eating style. In order to help you stay on your new, healthy course, sections have been included that deal with eating out and preparing holiday menus. The Brand Index will provide information for locating new or unfamiliar foods. Note that a nutritional analysis, quantifying per serving amounts of cholesterol, fat, saturated fat, and calories, plus diabetic exchanges follows each recipe.

These pages offer a variety of recipes, selected to appeal to your palate while satisfying many of the dietary specifications recommended for lowering blood cholesterol. You will see that you are allowed a large number of foods and that a low-cholesterol program need not be boring.

Shopping Guidelines

Americans are exercising more, smoking less, and starting to give thought to improving their diet by reducing or eliminating fat, sugar, sodium, and cholesterol. Learning which foods to choose from each of the four basic food groups and which ones to eliminate will protect the whole family.

The Meat Counter

You can still enjoy red meat, but not so often. You should choose cuts that are well trimmed and low in fat content. Buy leaner, less tender cuts with less marbling. Trim the visible fat before cooking. Pounding or braising the meat makes it tender. In addition, begin to add more poultry, especially turkey, to your diet. Organ meats (liver, kidney, brains) are very high in cholesterol.

For hamburgers, chili, and any other recipe that calls for ground beef, consider using ground veal or turkey instead. Both have less fat than ground beef. Turkey breast, for example, has a mere trace of fat—under 4 percent. Note: This figure does not include the skin or dark meat. Turkey skin contains more that 39 percent fat; dark meat averages over 8 percent.

Another terrific protein source is chicken. While chicken is low in cholesterol, remember that dark meat contains more fat than white meat. Chicken breasts are great because you can prepare them so many different ways. Just be sure to remove the skin from poultry before cooking it. Eliminate duck or goose because they contain very high levels of fat. Use them for a very special occasion, if at all.

Breads and Cereals

Most breads are low in fat and cholesterol. But if they are made with eggs or an excessive amount of butter or shortening, the fat and cholesterol contents may be too high. Watch out for brands that contain "partially hydrogenated fats." Croissants, puff pastry, and biscuits are examples of breads you will need to limit because of the fat content. If you are choosing bagels, select the water bagels rather than egg bagels.

Pasta is usually made with flour and water, but egg noodles contain egg yolks. Look for the new "no-yolk" noodles. They are delicious and good for you.

Packaged cake and dessert mixes are also made with egg yolks. Your best bet is to make your own. You will find several recipes in this book that you can adapt to fit your needs.

When it comes to breakfast cereals, fat and cholesterol are not usually a problem. Here, the culprit is usually sugar. If you are trying to make the healthiest choice, select oatmeal and wheat cereals. Avoid the popular granola bars because most are nothing more than candy bars that are high in fat.

Significant "Others"

Choose "buds" or powder that can be used in place of butter; they don't have any cholesterol. You will even find them flavored with sour cream and chives. Great on popcorn!

Choose olive oil and peanut oil, which reduce cholesterol levels. Always use a vegetable cooking spray to saute meat or vegetables; you can even find a butter-flavored spray now. Learn to make your own salad dressings because most of the prepared ones contain large amounts of fat. Check the labels.

Enjoy the rich taste of sour cream without the fat and cholesterol by substituting non-fat yogurt. Instead of heavy cream, use canned evaporated skimmed milk or non-fat dry milk. You can whip this, and if you add a dash of sugar, honey, or vanilla, it is delicious. Buttermilk is a good alternative to whole milk in cakes and cookies.

Beans, Nuts, and Seeds

Dried beans such as lentils, navy beans, pinto beans, garbanzos, and kidney beans offer a large amount of protein and have been shown to reduce cholesterol levels. Use them in new ways such as in salads, dips, and soups.

Most nuts and seeds primarily contain polyunsaturated or monounsaturated fats but no cholesterol. While they do provide some protein and carbohydrates, they are high in total fat and calories. Plain dried or dry-roasted nuts have less fat than oil-roasted nuts.

Fruits and Vegetables

Fruits and vegetables contain little fat and no cholesterol, and they are relatively low in calories. Another important fact about fruits and vegetables is that they are high in vitamins and minerals as well as dietary fiber. The only two fruits you will need to limit are avocados and olives because both are high in calories and total fat content. Small servings of these are recommended, or use them only for garnish.

The Dairy Case

While eggs are an excellent source of protein, egg yolks are one of the major sources of dietary cholesterol. The whites provide protein with no cholesterol. Consider egg substitutes that are fat free. Be sure to check the labels.

While calcium rich dairy foods are an important part of a balanced diet, we can certainly do without their fat and cholesterol. One way to begin to reduce your fat intake is to substitute low-fat milk (4.7 grams of fat per 8 ounces) for whole milk (9 grams). Ultimately, if you move to skim milk, you will be looking at only a trace of fat.

Cheese is another area where today's products can help you reduce fat. One cup of creamed cottage cheese has 9.5 grams of fat, but the 2 percent type has only 4.4 grams. By eating 1 percent cottage, you can cut your fat intake down to 2.3 grams per cup. Mozzarella cheese, an integral part of many recipes, contains 6.1 grams of fat per ounce, but the part-skim variety lowers the fat content to 4.8 grams. A good tip is to add the flavor of cheese without adding much fat by sprinkling grated Parmesan cheese. One tablespoon has only 1.5 grams of fat.

Yogurt requires our attention because there is a big difference between brands. Low-fat yogurt has about 3.4 grams of fat per cup. Non-fat brands have a mere 0.4 grams. Whole milk yogurts have 7.7 grams per 8-ounce container. Add your own fruit to low-fat or non-fat for a delicious treat.

Here are four more healthful tips: 1) Enjoy the rich taste of sour cream without the fat and cholesterol by substituting non-fat yogurt; 2) instead of heavy cream, use canned evaporated skimmed milk or non-fat dry milk—you can whip this, and if you add a dash of sugar, honey, or vanilla, it is delicious; 3) buttermilk is a good alternative to whole milk in cakes and cookies; 4) switch to non-dairy creamer to lighten your coffee, but be sure to choose one made with soy bean oil rather than palm or coconut oil, which are high in saturated fat (see Brand Index).

Fish

Fatty fish such as salmon, mackerel, and sardines are excellent choices because research shows that oily coldwater fish actually lowers cholesterol levels in people who eat it often. Most people enjoy canned tuna in salads or sandwiches. Consider adding canned salmon to these same menus. Just be sure to buy canned fish in spring water instead of oil.

The good news about shellfish is that except for shrimp, previous figures for cholesterol content were largely exaggerated and have been revised. For most people an occasional shrimp dish will not cause a problem. The all-time best choice in seafood is the versatile scallop.

If you buy fish frozen and breaded, be sure to read the labels carefully. Many batters are made with egg yolks and a lot of fat; others do not have egg yolks and contain relatively little fat.

Luncheon Meats

Luncheon meats are least desirable because even when they are made from turkey or chicken, they often contain an unhealthy amount of sodium and fat. A better choice is sliced turkey breast. Hot dogs and bologna, American favorites, are high in fat, saturated fat, cholesterol, and sodium. Consider switching to turkey dogs and meats made from lean turkey as these will be much lower in fat than the traditional choices. When you add the condiments usually chosen for hot dogs, you will not be able to tell the difference.

Breakfast Meats

Bacon and sausage have far too much fat and contain large amounts of sodium. One slice of Canadian bacon, on the other hand, has only 2 grams of fat.

Oils

When you are choosing a cooking oil, the most important health consideration is the amount of saturated fat. Products made with vegetable oil are not necessarily free of it. An oil low in saturated fat is, of course, more healthful. Coconut and palm oils contain the most saturated fat and are poor choices. Other vegetable oils contain saturated fats in much lower levels. Choose one of those listed below and use in moderation.

Do not be fooled into thinking that a bottle of vegetable oil with a "no cholesterol" label is better for you. All vegetable oils are cholesterol free. Only animal fats contain cholesterol. If an oil is low in saturated fat, it's not important whether or not most of the remaining fat is monounsaturated or polyunsaturated. In fact, many health authorities encourage a mix. Both corn oil (mostly polyunsaturated) and olive oil (mostly monounsaturated) can have a healthful place in your diet.

Considerations such as flavor, cost, and cooking performance should influence your buying decisions. I prefer olive oil for a more robust flavor. Corn oil is a good choice for oriental cooking and for those dishes with a more delicate flavor.

Check labels. A label may say "100 percent vegetable shortening," but the ingredient listing may show that the vegetable shortening contains coconut or palm oil.

Choose any of the following oils:		*Avoid the following oils:*
Safflower	Soybean	Palm
Corn	Olive	Palm kernel
	Peanut	Coconut

Cooking Suggestions

You've gone shopping and your kitchen is now stocked with great-tasting, low-saturated-fat, low-cholesterol foods. But you may still be tempted to prepare rich soups, breads, and high-fat goodies. The suggestions below will help you to reduce the amount of total and saturated fats in these foods. Remember, roasting, baking, broiling, braising, and sauteing are recommended cooking methods for meat, fish, and poultry because they require adding little additional fat in the cooking process.

How To Reduce Saturated Fats in Cooking

* Trim meats of all visible fat.

* Roast or broil on a rack so fat can drain off.

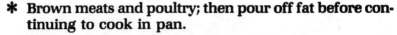

* Brown meats and poultry; then pour off fat before continuing to cook in pan.

* Baste meats with corn oil, wine, tomato juice, or lemon juice instead of fatty drippings.

* Make pot roasts and stews a day ahead. Chill and remove the fat that has formed on top before reheating.

* Avoid prolonged soaking of fresh vegetables, and don't wash rice before cooking in order to preserve water-soluble vitamins.

* Prepare salads just before they are to be served. Avoid cutting and cooking vegetables until the last minute. This reduces loss of vitamin C.

* Steam vegetables instead of deep frying.

* Bake, grill, or broil meats instead of frying.

* Use polyunsaturated oils or an air popper when popping corn.

* Serve entrees on a bed or rice or pasta instead of with egg noodles.

* Poach fish in vegetable broth to retain moisture and limit fat.

* Marinate meats in wine and herbs and spices instead of using gravies.

* Saute vegetables and meats in vegetable sprays, margarine, or polyunsaturated oils instead of butter.

* Make scalloped potatoes using skim milk and margarine instead of whole milk and butter.

* Use tub margarine instead of stick margarine to help limit saturated fat.

* Make your own breakfast yogurt by adding oats, raisins, and cinnamon to low-fat plain yogurt.

* Eat chicken and turkey without the skin to reduce saturated fat.

* Add oats to meatloaf and hamburgers instead of breadcrumbs.

* Cream soups with skim milk.

How to Adapt Your Recipes

You can prepare delicious meals with less fat and cholesterol, as well as fewer calories, using these substitutions.

Original Ingredient	Substitution	Use For
⅔ cup whipping cream	2 egg whites	Mousses
1 cup whipping cream	Mock whipped cream	Creams
1 cup whole milk	1 cup skim milk 1 cup buttermilk Non-fat dry milk	Cakes
8 ounces cream cheese	8 ounces part-skim ricotta cheese	Cheesecakes
Sour cream	Low-fat yogurt	Cookies Muffins
2 whole eggs	2 egg whites + 1 yolk or egg substitute to equal 2 eggs	Cakes, Custards
Chocolate	Cocoa blended with veg. oil or margarine (1 1-oz. square of chocolate = 3 tablespoons of cocoa + 1 tablespoon oil or margarine)	Cakes, Cookies
Butter	Margarine or oil (1 tablespoon butter = 1 tablespoon margarine or ¾ tablespoon oil)	Cakes, Puddings, Frostings

Holiday Menus

Holiday celebrations need not mean the downfall of your diet because the menus are composed of rich foods and all the things you have been avoiding. You don't have to resist the urge to sample everything on the table when you have chosen recipes from this book. The following menus are meant as suggestions and will probably remind you of some of your own favorites. If a recipe you love is not in the book, look in the preceding section to see if there is a low-fat substitute you can use to bring the recipe in line with your new way of eating.

When you plan your meals, select dishes with attractive colors that will be eye-appealing as well as flavors that

Note: Recipes for all of the following dishes are included in this book; see Index. Look under "key word" if not found under first word.

complement one another and textures that form a contrast. Before the occasion, spend some time planning the center-piece, china, and linens you will use. These will lend a festive air to your meal, and guests will know that you cared enough to take time to plan the event right down to the last detail. Your reward for all this work will be the compliments you receive from family and friends.

Thanksgiving

Cheese-Stuffed Mushrooms
Seafood Pasta Soup
The Best Roasted Chicken (or Turkey)
Baked Acorn Squash
Spinach Salad
Alicia's Holiday Cranberry Sauce
Pavlova

A Very Special Dinner

Parsley Soup
Scallops à la Mushrooms
Garlic Mashed Potatoes
Peas French Style
Devonshire Cream

Spring Luncheon

Vichyssoise
Salade Nicoise
Divine Chocolate Angel Food Cake with
   Raspberries

Light Supper

Tomato Aspic
Terrific Caesar Salad
Peach Blueberry Crisp

A Vegetarian Feast

Tabouleh
Spinach Soup
Asparagus Pie
Stuffed Cabbage Leaves
Apple Flan

The Elegant Brunch

Iced Mocha Coffee
Apple Raisin Muffins
Strawberry Cottage Cheese Crepes
Bagels
Honey Orange Spread
Melon Balls Supreme

"After the Game" Supper

Hummus
Vegetarian Minestrone
All American Meat Loaf
Twice Baked Potatoes
Confetti Corn Casserole
Crunchy Broccoli Salad
Chocolate Cupcake Surprise

Spring Has Arrived

Artichoke Dip
Asparagus Salad Supreme
Baked Fish with Tomato Basil Sauce
Strawberry-Almond Shortcake

Greek Festival

Artichoke Dip with Veggies
Greek Lemon Soup
Moussaka
Tomatoes Stuffed with Beans
Lemon Sponge Cake

Chinese Delight

Stuffed Celery
Chinese Hot Pot
Chinese Coleslaw
Beef and Mushroom Stir-Fry
Apple Rice Pudding

Dinner with a Mexican Twist

Spanish Gazpacho
Vegetarian Chili
Sombreros (Taco Salad)
Tangy Lemon Mousse

Italian Feast

Melon Balls in Lambrusco
Italian Bean Soup
Vegetable-Stuffed Shells
Salade Provencale
Tortoni

Elegant French Dinner

French Onion Soup
Vegetable Caviar
Boeuf Bourguignon
Asparagus with Mustard Cream Sauce
Pears Belle Helene

Country French Picnic

Mushroom Pate
Caponata with Pita Bread
Onion Tart
Basque Tomatoes
Seafood Pasta Salad
Parisian Sable Cookies

Outdoor Barbecue

Heart-Healthy Deviled Eggs
Deviled Dogs
La Poet Potato Salad
Divine Cucumber Salad
Brownies

St. Patrick's Day Bash

Cream of Pea Soup
Very Special Beef Stew
Parsley and Garbanzo Bean Salad
Irish Coffee Parfait

Easter Sunday Dinner

Salmon-Filled Mushroom Caps
Asparagus Vinaigrette
Herb-Scented Leg of Lamb
Peas French Style
Cherry Cheesecake

Valentine's Day

Surprise the one you love with this breakfast or dinner!

BREAKFAST:
Carrot Mary
Salmon Flan
Strawberries Barbara
Cherry Yogurt Cream Muffins

DINNER:
Tomatoes with Mozzarella and Basil
Court Salad
Salmon Loaf with Two Sauces
Mushrooms Normandy
Coeur à la Crème with Strawberries

When You Dine Out

One of my favorite pastimes is to dine out. I love the change of scenery and the chance to spend time with friends. We often choose a new restaurant to try, or we patronize our old favorites.

Today, Americans are dining out more often, both as a luxury and as a necessity. Even though you are on a low-cholesterol diet, there is no reason to give up dining out. You need it for your emotional well being. If you follow the guidelines listed below, you can still enjoy a good restaurant meal and stay on your healthy heart program.

First, you should call the restaurant and get an idea of what kind of food they serve and if special requests will be honored. Questions to ask when you call, or in person if calling is not possible, include the following, each preceded by the phrase, "Do You":

1. Serve margarine (rather than butter) with the meal?
2. Serve skim (rather than whole) milk?
3. Omit MSG when cooking your order?
4. Steam vegetables rather than serving them in a butter sauce?
5. Broil, bake, steam, or poach meat, fish, or poultry?
6. Have a special seating area for non-smokers?
7. Offer low-calorie sweeteners instead of sugar?
8. Leave all butter, gravy, or sauce off a dish?
9. Offer fresh fruit or canned fruit in light syrup for dessert?

   Once you arrive at the restaurant, prepare to be assertive. Remember, you are the patron. Do not allow yourself to be intimidated by the menu, waiter, or waitress. You can order anything you want, even an appetizer as a main dish if you are interested in reduced portions. Insist that the food be served the way you want it, with sauces and dressings on the side. Don't be afraid to ask questions.

✓ Tips on Reading Menus

Learn how to recognize low-fat preparation. Look for these descriptions:

Steamed

Poached

Garden fresh

Broiled

In spring water

Roasted

Beware of the following terms:

In butter sauce	Creamed
Sauteed	Au gratin
Fried	Escalloped
In cream sauce	In cheese sauce
Stewed	Casserole
Hash	

If you are trying to limit your sodium intake, beware of the following:

Pickled

Smoked

In broth

✓ Foods To Order

Breakfast

Order fresh fruit or a small glass of juice to start. Always request whole-grain bread or an English muffin toasted dry with margarine served on the side. If the restaurant is willing, cinnamon toast made with margarine is delicious. If you are ordering cereal, be sure to ask for oatmeal or those made from whole grains. You will also need to request skim or low-fat milk for your cereal or to have with your coffee or tea. You can also order a vegetable omelet made only with egg whites. I find more and more restaurants willing to do this. You can also consider a waffle topped with fresh fruit.

Beverages

If you wish to have a cocktail, be aware that alcohol adds calories. You'll want your liquor mixed with water, juice, or low-calorie soda or seltzer instead of pre-sweetened mixes. A wine spritzer is a good choice. Just add seltzer to a glass of wine. Best of all are non-alcoholic drinks such as fruit juice mixed with club soda or club soda with a twist of lemon or lime. Tomato or V8 juice is another refreshing alternative.

Bread

My favorite Italian restaurant now makes my beloved garlic bread with margarine. I love them. You can enjoy bread just as long as you resist the high-fat spreads.

Appetizers

Tomato juice, V8 juice, clear broth, bouillon, consomme, shrimp or crabmeat cocktail, salads, and raw vegetables are all fine.

Meat, Poultry, Fish

Request that these be roasted, baked, or broiled, without skin in the case of poultry. Ask for lemon instead of butter for your seafood.

Eggs

Many restaurants now serve Egg Beaters; be sure to ask. Otherwise, your only alternative is omelets made of only egg whites.

Potatoes and Such

Boiled new potatoes and baked potatoes are the best choices. Avoid the butter. Avoid noodles; they are made with egg yolks. Rice is always a good substitute.

Fats

Avoid butter, sour cream, creamy salad dressings and those with cheese. Ask for these on the side so you can control how much you use.

Salads

Vegetable, lettuce, tomato, cottage cheese, tuna, chicken, fish, potato, macaroni, rice, and bean are all excellent choices. Avoid chef salad with cold cuts and cheese and Greek salad with feta cheese, anchovies, and olives.

Vegetables

Steamed, broiled, or salad bar vegetables can be eaten in unlimited quantities. Always ask if vegetables are available because you can often substitute them for potatoes if you are counting calories.

Desserts

Choose fresh fruit, fruit ices, sherbets, gelatin, or angel food cake. An elegant finish to a gourmet meal is espresso or demitasse, black with a twist of orange or lemon.

✓Fast Foods

The U.S.A. is now dotted with fast food restaurants eager for our business. Unfortunately, most fast food places do not offer the kind of food diet-conscious Americans are looking for. There are some exceptions because the chains are beginning to respond to requests for things such as salad bars, pasta bars, and baked potato entrees.

If you are in the habit of eating in fast food restaurants, I would like to recommend that you purchase the American Diabetes Association Family Cookbook. It includes a listing of all the major fast food chains in the country with their top-selling items and lists all the nutritional information you need to make intelligent decisions for your family. I firmly believe that we need to communicate with these restaurants in order to be offered the kind of food we want.

✓The Brown Bag Lunch

We all tote food for one occasion or another be it school, work, or a picnic. A low-cholesterol diet can be adapted to eating anywhere. Ideally, you want to avoid the need to purchase food from vending machines and the like because they will never be able to provide the meals your program demands.

The first investment you will need to make is the purchase of a vacuum bottle for taking along hot drinks, soups, and main dishes such as chili, stew, or a salad to add variety. Lunch can be much more than just a sandwich. With a little imagination, you can bring along meals that others will envy. Vary your sandwiches with pita, whole-wheat, or rye breads.

In addition to sandwiches, consider the following salads and soups:

West Coast Salad	Garlic Vegetable Soup
Oriental Chicken Salad	Lentil Soup
Rotini Salad	French Onion Soup
Parsley and Garbanzo Bean Salad	Cream of Pea Soup
Golden Gate Salad	Cabbage Soup
Divine Cucumber Salad	Greek Lemon Soup

Fresh fruit and homemade cookies will be a nice ending to any portable luncheon or picnic.

Note: Recipes for all of the above dishes are included in this book; see Index. Look under "key word" if not found under first word.

Appetizers

Nothing makes parties more festive or special occasions more special than trays laden with eye-appealing appetizers. My mother loved to serve appetizers and searched for decorative and imaginative ways to display them. Sometimes a dip came to the table in a red, green, or yellow pepper. Sometimes she would fill an artichoke with dip, especially a warm one. Everything had to look beautiful as well as taste delicious.

Appetizers should whet the appetite, not dull it, and they should be selected according to the meal that will follow. Serve a light appetizer with a hearty meal and a larger selection of appetizers with a light meal. The following collection of appetizers offers you a vast choice of taste-tempting treats.

Some appetizers are hot, others cold. You can serve bowls of crackers with vegetables and a delicious dip. Cheese, horseradish, onions, beans, and cucumbers all lend distinctive tastes to luscious, creamy dips. There is no limit to the choices you have available.

Some of these special treats are sure to be popular with the special people in your life. There are some tiny meat treats and some spectacular seafood specialties. Serve your appetizers with pride and wait for the compliments, which are sure to follow.

✳
Stuffed Celery

6 celery stalks, washed with leaves removed
1 cup low-fat cottage cheese
¼ cup scallions, chopped
2 teaspoons lemon juice
½ teaspoon Tamari soy sauce
1 teaspoon prepared mustard
¼ cup pimiento, chopped
¼ cup chives, chopped
1 garlic clove, minced

Place cottage cheese and all ingredients except celery in a blender. Blend till smooth. Stuff celery with cheese mixture. Cut each stalk into 6 individual pieces. Serve each with a toothpick. Makes 36 appetizers, or 6 servings of 6 each.

PER SERVING:
Cholesterol (mg): 0
Fat (grams): total 1; saturated 0
Exchanges: milk 0; fruit 0; bread/starch 0;
vegetable 1; meat 0; fat 0
Calories: 36

Italian Bruschetta
Broiled Italian bread with tomatoes, olives, cheese, and basil

> 1 long, slender loaf of crisp-crusted Italian bread
> 3 large garlic cloves, peeled and cut in half
> 4 tablespoons olive oil
> 2 cups tomatoes, diced
> ¼ cup olive oil
> ½ cup black olives, sliced
> ¼ cup red wine vinegar
> ½ cup green onions, chopped
> 2 cups part-skim mozzarella cheese, shredded
> ½ cup fresh basil leaves, minced

Split loaf in half. Grill, cut side down, over medium-hot barbecue fire or under broiler until lightly toasted. Rub toasted side with garlic clove well. Brush with olive oil. Cut each half of bread crosswise into four equal portions, making a total of 8 pieces.

For salad, place remaining ingredients except basil in a bowl and mix well. Cover bread with salad; top with basil. Place under the broiler just until cheese melts. Serves 4.

PER SERVING:
Cholesterol (mg): 32
Fat (grams): total 29; saturated 9
Exchanges: milk 0; fruit 0; bread/starch 2; vegetable 0; meat 2; fat 4
Calories: 462

Artichoke Dip

> 28 ozs. canned artichokes, drained and chopped
> ½ cup mock sour cream
> 2 cups low-fat yogurt

1½ cups Parmesan cheese, grated
3 tablespoons scallions, chopped
2 tablespoons chives, chopped
4 tablespoons Marsala wine

In small bowl, combine all ingredients. Mix well. Spoon mixture into a greased casserole. Bake in preheated 375° oven 30 minutes or until golden brown. Serve immediately with crackers, vegetables, or black bread. Serves 10.

PER SERVING:
Cholesterol (mg): 10
Fat (grams): total 10; saturated 2
Exchanges: milk 0; fruit 0; bread/starch 0;
vegetable 1; meat 1; fat 1
Calories: 104

Hummus

2 15½ oz. cans garbanzo beans
1 tablespoon lemon juice
6–8 cloves garlic
3 tablespoons olive oil
½ cup parsley, chopped
Pita bread triangles

In food processor or blender, blend 1 can garbanzo beans with liquid and one can drained with lemon juice and garlic. Blend till smooth. Place mixture in bowl and pour olive oil over top. Sprinkle with parsley. Serve with pita bread triangles for dipping. Serves 10.

PER SERVING:
Cholesterol (mg): 0
Fat (grams): total 6; saturated 4
Exchanges: milk 0; fruit 0; bread/starch 2;
vegetable 0; meat 0; fat 1
Calories: 194 Note: Does not include calories from
pita bread triangles.

✳
Mushroom Pate

Vegetable cooking spray
½ lb. margarine
2 lbs. mushrooms, finely chopped
¾ teaspoon Spike
 Pepper, freshly ground to taste
 Egg substitute to equal 3 eggs
1 tablespoon skim milk

Spray 3-cup mold with vegetable cooking spray.

In heavy skillet, melt margarine. Add mushrooms. Cook over low heat, stirring frequently until liquid evaporates and mushrooms brown, about 35 minutes. Season with Spike and pepper. Remove from heat.

In separate bowl mix egg substitute with skim milk. To this, add 3 tablespoons mushroom mixture. Mix well. Combine egg mixture with mushrooms in skillet. Cook over low heat 2 to 3 minutes, stirring constantly.

Pour into mold. Chill until firm. Unmold and serve at room temperature with crackers. Serves 10.

PER SERVING:
Cholesterol (mg): 0
Fat (grams): total 10; saturated 2
Exchanges: milk 0; fruit 0; bread/starch 0;
vegetable 1; meat 0; fat 2
Calories: 113

✳

Small Cocktail Quiche

2 egg whites
1 egg yolk
1 lb. low-fat cottage cheese
3 tablespoons mock sour cream
4 ozs. Lorraine cheese, chopped well
½ cup Bisquick
   Pepper to taste
4 tablespoons butter or margarine, melted
   Vegetable cooking spray

In large bowl, combine all ingredients. Blend until just mixed. Spray miniature muffin cups liberally with vegetable spray. Fill each cup ⅞ full. Bake in preheated 375° oven 25–30 minutes. Cool in cups before removing. Reheat 10 minutes before serving. Makes 5 dozen. Two quiches per serving.

PER SERVING:
Cholesterol (mg): 14
Fat (grams): total 4; saturated 0
Exchanges: milk 0; fruit 0; bread/starch 0;
vegetable 0; meat 0; fat 1
Calories: 52

Scallops in Mustard-Dill Sauce

2½ lbs. bay scallops, uncooked
2 tablespoons margarine
3 tablespoons all-purpose flour
1 cup chicken broth
1 cup skim milk
¼ cup Dijon-style mustard
1 teaspoon lemon juice
White pepper, dash
½ cup fresh dill, chopped

Poach scallops in simmering water until just opaque. Do not overcook. Rinse under cold water to stop cooking process. Drain and refrigerate.

Melt margarine in medium-size saucepan. Stir in flour and cook 1 minute. Add chicken broth and skim milk, stirring constantly with a whisk. Bring to a boil. Lower heat and simmer 5 minutes, stirring occasionally. Remove from heat and whisk in mustard, lemon juice, and pepper. Stir in dill.

Refrigerate at least 2 hours. Before serving, mix scallops with mustard sauce. Serve on lettuce-lined plates or in small coquille shells. Serves 8.

PER SERVING:
Cholesterol (mg): 49
Fat (grams): total 3; saturated 0
Exchanges: milk 0; fruit 0; bread/starch 0;
vegetable 0; meat 3; fat 0
Calories: 162

Cheese-Stuffed Mushrooms

16 large fresh mushrooms
2 tablespoons green onion, sliced
2 teaspoons margarine
½ cup low-fat cottage cheese
1½ teaspoons prepared mustard
½ teaspoon Worcestershire sauce

Remove stems from mushrooms; chop stems. Set mushroom caps aside. Cook chopped stems and onion in margarine until vegetables are tender and liquid is absorbed. Remove from heat. Combine cottage cheese, mustard, and Worcestershire sauce. Add cooked mushroom mixture; mix well.

Fill mushroom caps with mixture. Place on baking sheet; bake in 375° oven 8–10 minutes or until tender. Drain on paper toweling. Makes 16 appetizers, or 4 servings of 4 mushrooms each.

PER SERVING:
Cholesterol (mg): Less than 1
Fat (grams): total 2; saturated less than 1
Exchanges: milk 0; fruit 0; bread/starch 0;
vegetable 1; meat 0; fat ½
Calories: 52

※

Vegetable Caviar

1 small eggplant, peeled
1 small acorn squash, halved and seeded
3 large green bell peppers
1 medium head cauliflower, leaves removed
1 bunch broccoli, leaves removed and stems
   sliced
1 tablespoon garlic, finely chopped
3 tablespoons lemon juice
¼ cup white wine
6 tablespoons olive oil
4 tablespoons fresh parsley, finely chopped

Preheat oven to 475°. Place vegetables in baking dish. Bake 30 minutes and remove all vegetables except acorn squash and eggplant. Bake squash and eggplant 15 minutes longer.

After cooking, chop the green peppers. Cut eggplant into cubes. Scoop pulp from squash. Chop cauliflower and broccoli. Combine all vegetables in a medium-size bowl. Chop and mix thoroughly until mixture is well combined. Add garlic, lemon juice, wine, olive oil, and parsley. Blend thoroughly. Chill at least 2 hours before serving. Serve this with slices of black bread. Serves 8–10.

PER SERVING (one serving includes one slice of bread):
Cholesterol (mg): less than 1
Fat (grams): total 9; saturated less than 1
Exchanges: milk 0; fruit 0; bread/starch 1; vegetable 3; meat 0; fat 2
Calories: 230

Tabouleh

This recipe must be made with fresh mint; dried will not work

1 cup bulghur wheat
2 cups boiling water
½ cup scallions, chopped
5 tablespoons fresh mint, chopped
2 medium-size tomatoes, seeded and chopped
1 cup fresh parsley, chopped
5 tablespoons olive oil
6 tablespoons fresh lemon juice
10 large lettuce leaves

Put bulghur into a bowl and add boiling water. Stir, cover bowl, and let stand 35 minutes. Drain, squeezing out any remaining water between the palms of your hands. Put into a serving bowl. Add scallions, mint, tomatoes, and parsley. Toss gently. Add olive oil. Stir until well mixed. Add lemon juice and stir again until well mixed.

You can serve the tabouleh in a serving bowl or on individual plates. Use lettuce leaves as scoops to eat the tabouleh. Serves 10.

PER SERVING:
Cholesterol (mg): 0
Fat (grams): total 91; saturated 1
Exchanges: milk 0; fruit 0; bread/starch ½;
vegetable 0; meat 0; fat 2
Calories: 115

Onion Tart

4 tablespoons margarine
¼ cup white wine
½ teaspoon dried dill
2 garlic cloves, quartered
6 large onions, coarsely chopped
¼ cup chives, minced
3 tablespoons sugar
1½ cups breadcrumbs
1 cup matzoh, crumbled
1 cup part-skim mozzarella, shredded

Melt 3 tablespoons margarine in a large saucepan and add wine, dill, and garlic. Reduce heat to low and add onions, chives, and sugar. Stir gently until sugar has completely dissolved. Simmer another 5 minutes. Remove saucepan from heat.

Preheat oven to 375°. Grease 9-in. pie pan with remaining margarine. Spoon thin layer of onion mixture into pan. Cover with thin layer of breadcrumbs and crumbled matzoh. Repeat process until onion, breadcrumbs, and matzoh are used up.

Top tart with mozzarella cheese, and bake 15 minutes or until cheese is melted and lightly browned. Remove tart from oven, cut into squares or wedges, and serve hot. Serves 6.

PER SERVING:
Cholesterol (mg): 21
Fat (grams): total 15; saturated 5
Exchanges: milk 0; fruit 0; bread/starch 3;
vegetable 0; meat 2; fat 2
Calories: 418

Marinated Mushrooms and Artichoke Hearts

1 cup olive oil
2 tablespoons tarragon vinegar
2 tablespoons vermouth
4 tablespoons lemon juice
1 teaspoon dried basil leaves, crushed
½ teaspoon dry mustard
2 cloves garlic, crushed
1 lb. small button mushrooms
1 15-oz. can artichoke hearts
½ cup black olives, minced
¼ cup pimiento, diced
½ cup parsley, snipped
   Boston lettuce leaves

Combine olive oil, vinegar, vermouth, lemon juice, basil, dry mustard, and garlic in a large bottle with a tight-fitting lid. Shake well. Put mushrooms, artichoke hearts, olives, pimiento, and parsley into a bowl. Pour dressing over vegetables and mix well. Arrange lettuce leaves on a platter and spoon marinated vegetables onto lettuce leaves. Place in refrigerator 2 hours before serving. When ready to serve, place toothpicks alongside platter. Serves 12.

PER SERVING:
Cholesterol (mg): 0
Fat (grams): total 20; saturated 3
Exchanges: milk 0; fruit 0; bread/starch 0;
vegetable 1; meat 0; fat 4
Calories: 208

Baked Stuffed Tomatoes

8 tomatoes, seeded and pulp removed (reserve
   pulp)
1 garlic clove, chopped
1 tablespoon parsley, chopped
1 tablespoon basil, chopped
3 tablespoons dry white wine
2 tablespoons olive oil
¼ cup Italian breadcrumbs
½ cup part-skim mozzarella cheese, shredded
   Parsley for garnish

Preheat oven to 425°. With a fork, mix tomato pulp
with chopped garlic, parsley, and basil in a medium-size
mixing bowl. Combine wine and olive oil and blend into
mixture. Add breadcrumbs and mix well. Spoon into each
tomato shell.

Spray a large baking dish with vegetable cooking spray
and arrange tomatoes in it. Bake about 10 minutes. Remove
dish and top each tomato with some mozzarella cheese.
Return to oven and bake another 10 minutes until cheese
is melted and lightly golden in color. Garnish with parsley. Serves 8.

PER SERVING:
Cholesterol (mg): 8
Fat (grams): total 6; saturated 2
Exchanges: milk 0; fruit 0; bread/starch 0;
vegetable 2; meat 0; fat 1
Calories: 118

Melon Balls in Lambrusco
(sparkling red wine)

4 cantaloupes
2 cups Lambrusco (sparkling red wine)
½ cup maraschino cherries
2 seedless oranges, quartered and sliced thin
8 thin slices lemon
8 fresh mint leaves

Cut melons into halves; discard seeds. With a melon-ball cutter, make melon balls and place in large bowl. Reserve melon shells for refilling. Pour Lambrusco over melon balls and allow to marinate at room temperature 20 minutes. Stir, cover bowl, and place in refrigerator to chill 2 hours.

Remove from refrigerator and blend in maraschino cherries. Then put melon ball mixture back into shells. Garnish with orange, lemon, and mint. Serves 8.

PER SERVING:
Cholesterol (mg): 0
Fat (grams): total 0; saturated 0
Exchanges: milk 0; fruit 0; bread/starch 1;
vegetable 0; meat 0; fat 0
Calories: 87

Tomatoes with Mozzarella and Basil

4 tomatoes
    Lettuce leaves, red leaves preferable
3 tablespoons olive oil
1 teaspoon dry white wine
½ teaspoon oregano
½ teaspoon fresh basil
1 lb. part-skim mozzarella cheese, shredded
    Fresh basil leaves (optional)

Cut tomatoes into slices. Divide tomato slices into 4 individual servings and place on salad plates with lettuce leaves. Blend oil, wine, and seasonings. Drizzle over tomatoes. Sprinkle cheese on top. You can add fresh basil leaves for garnish. Serves 4.

PER SERVING:
Cholesterol (mg): 30
Fat (grams): total 15; saturated 6
Exchanges: milk 0; fruit 0; bread/starch 0;
vegetable 1; meat 2; fat 2
Calories: 214

Salmon-Filled Mushroom Caps

1 7½-oz. can salmon without bones
2 tablespoons fine dry breadcrumbs
2 tablespoons green onion, finely chopped
2 tablespoons parsley, snipped
18 1½–2-in. fresh mushroom caps, washed and
    well drained
2 tablespoons canned pimiento, diced
3 tablespoons margarine, melted

In a small mixing bowl, combine salmon, breadcrumbs, green onion, and snipped parsley.
Remove mushroom stems from caps; reserve stems

for another recipe. Place mushroom caps in a 15x10x1-in. baking pan, crown side down. Mound salmon mixture into caps. Place a little pimiento on top of each cap. Cover and chill 3–24 hours.

To serve, uncover, drizzle with margarine, and bake at 350° for 15–20 minutes or until tender. Makes 18 appetizers or 6 servings of 3 mushrooms each.

PER SERVING:
Cholesterol (mg): 12
Fat (grams): total 10; saturated 1
Exchanges: milk 0; fruit 0; bread/starch 0;
vegetable 1; meat 1; fat 2
Calories: 147

Heart-Healthy Deviled Eggs

8 eggs, hard boiled, cut in half, yolks removed
½ cup low-fat cottage cheese
¼ cup light mayonnaise
¼ cup green onion, finely minced
¼ cup celery, finely minced
¼ teaspoon celery seed
¼ teaspoon Spike
1 teaspoon Dijon mustard
2 tablespoons parsley, minced

In medium bowl, beat cottage cheese and mayonnaise until fluffy. Add remaining ingredients and beat well. Stuff hard-boiled egg shells with the mixture and refrigerate. Before serving, dust with minced parsley. Serves 8 (2 deviled eggs each).

PER SERVING:
Cholesterol (mg): 0
Fat (grams): total 1; saturated 0
Exchanges: milk 0; fruit 0; bread/starch 0;
vegetable 0; meat ½; fat 0
Calories: 36

✳

Caponata

1 large eggplant
⅔ cup olive oil
5 cloves garlic, pressed
1 cup onions, chopped
½ cup green bell peppers, diced
½ cup celery, diced
1 black olives, halved and pitted
1 15½-oz. can Italian tomatoes with liquid, chopped
2 tablespoons capers
2 teaspoons oregano
1 teaspoon sweet basil
¼ teaspoon pepper
2 tablespoons roasted peppers, chopped
3 tablespoons wine vinegar
1 or 2 drops hot pepper sauce

Cube eggplant with skin on. Saute eggplant and garlic in olive oil until golden; remove from skillet. In same skillet, saute onion, green peppers, and celery until tender. Stir in remaining ingredients, along with eggplant, and simmer uncovered 20 minutes. Adjust seasoning. Cool, then chill. Serve at room temperature with pita bread triangles or water crackers. Serves 10.

PER SERVING:
Cholesterol (mg): 0
Fat (grams): total 16; saturated 2
Exchanges: milk 0; fruit 0; bread/starch 0;
vegetable 1; meat 0; fat 3
Calories: 180 (Does not include pita bread)

Soups

One of my fondest childhood memories was of the stock-pot my grandmother always kept on the stove. You cannot imagine the things that found their way into that pot. Tops of celery, vegetables that had lost their freshness, left-over meat; nothing was wasted when it could go into the stockpot.

Soups today are more easily made, but my grandmother believed that a soup is only as good as the broth it is made from. Soup was served in our home with nearly every meal. Whether it was the lightest lunch or the most elaborate dinner party, there was a suitable soup for the occasion. You can make a substantial soup such as Chicken-in-the-Pot for a winter supper, a vichyssoise for a small luncheon, gazpacho for a summer dinner party, or French onion soup for a formal dinner—the suggestions are almost endless.

Most of the soups in this chapter are made from vegetables and fruit, so they are excellent for anyone watching their cholesterol intake. Many are also low in calories.

A tureen is the best container in which to serve soup as it can be the centerpiece of your table and eliminates repeated trips to the kitchen to fill bowls or provide second helpings. I think it is nice to have two types of soup bowls, those with wide tops for the hearty soups, and small bouillon cups for the lighter, more delicate soups, especially those served in summer.

Beef Broth

 2 lbs. beef bones
 1 onion
 1 carrot
 1 turnip
 1 leek
10 cups water
 4 peppercorns
 ½ teaspoon meat extract

Wash the beef bones and trim off excess fat. Prepare the vegetables and chop them into large pieces. Place all ingredients in a large kettle. Bring the stock to a boil, cover, and simmer slowly 4–5 hours. Strain the stock. Either allow it to become cold and remove fat, or remove the fat with paper towels by pulling them across surface of the hot stock. Makes 2½ quarts.

Calories: 25 per serving

Turkey or Chicken Stock

12 cups water
3 lbs. chicken or turkey, uncooked
2 large onions, chopped
1 medium carrot, chopped
2 stalks celery with tops, chopped
4 peppercorns
4 cloves
1 tablespoon parsley
½ teaspoon basil

Remove skin from chicken or turkey. Place all ingredients in a large soup kettle and bring to a boil. Reduce heat to low and cook about 3½ hours. Skim foam from surface.

Remove from heat and remove chicken and vegetables with a slotted spoon. Strain broth, place in covered bowl, and refrigerate. Rinse chicken and vegetables and refrigerate in a covered dish.

Before serving, chop chicken into bite-size pieces and return it with vegetables to the broth after skimming fat from top. Heat just to boiling and remove from heat. Store until ready to use. Can be frozen. Makes 1½–2 quarts.

PER SERVING (one cup):
Cholesterol (mg): 1
Fat (grams): total 1; saturated 0
Exchanges: milk 0; fruit 0; bread/starch 0;
vegetable 0; meat ½; fat 1
Calories: 40 per serving

Garlic Vegetable Soup

5 tablespoons olive oil
1 cup leeks, finely chopped
5 garlic cloves
2½ quarts water
½ cup white beans, cooked
1 lb. fresh tomatoes, peeled, seeded, and
    coarsely chopped
1 cup new potatoes, diced
1 cup carrots, coarsely chopped
½ cup celery, chopped
1 cup fresh green beans, cut up
4 tablespoons dried basil
1 tablespoon tarragon
2 tablespoons tomato paste
Pepper, freshly ground

Heat 2 tablespoons olive oil in a large saucepan. Add leeks and garlic and saute over low heat for 5 minutes. Add remaining ingredients, including remaining olive oil, and simmer over medium heat 30 minutes, stirring occasionally. Serve hot. Serves 8.

PER SERVING:
Cholesterol (mg): 0
Fat (grams): total 9; saturated 1
Exchanges: milk 0; fruit 0; bread/starch 1;
vegetable 0; meat 0; fat 2
Calories: 150

✳ Lentil Soup

3 cups dried lentils
3 quarts cold water
½ lb. beef brisket, flank or stew meat
1 medium-size leek, finely chopped
3 large carrots, finely chopped
½ cup celery, chopped
1 cup onion, finely chopped
2 tablespoons flour
¼ cup white wine

Rinse and sort lentils under cold water. In a large pot, bring water to a boil. Add lentils, beef, leek, carrots, and celery. Return mixture to a boil, reduce heat, cover, and simmer for 40 minutes. Remove beef and brown in a skillet over low heat. When it is very hot, add onions. Cook 15 minutes, stirring frequently. Sprinkle flour over onions. Stir until flour browns. Pour 1 cup of lentil mixture over onions and stir vigorously. Add white wine and cook 1 minute longer. Add contents of skillet to lentils. Simmer 30 minutes. Serves 8.

PER SERVING:
Cholesterol (mg): 20
Fat (grams): total 3; saturated 1
Exchanges: milk 0; fruit 0; bread/starch 1;
vegetable 0; meat 1; fat 0
Calories: 125

✳
Chicken-in-the-Pot

5 lbs. chicken, whole
Water to cover
3½ quarts water
  1 large onion, studded with 1 whole clove
  8 medium-sized carrots, peeled
  6 leeks, washed and trimmed
  8 stalks celery
  8 sprigs parsley
  ½ cup mushrooms, sliced
  ½ lb. small white onions
  Rice, cooked (4 cups)

Clean chicken and truss legs and wings. Place in large soup kettle, add water to cover, and bring to a boil. Cook for a few minutes. Remove chicken and discard water. Wash kettle and return chicken. Cover chicken with 3½ quarts water, and skim scum that rises to surface as you bring water to a boil. When no more scum appears, simmer chicken, covered, for 1 hour.

Peel onion, stud with clove, and add to chicken together with 1 of the carrots, 2 leeks, 2 celery stalks, and ½ the parsley. Continue to simmer the soup for another hour. Correct seasonings. Remove chicken and set aside to keep warm.

Using a fine sieve, strain soup into a clean kettle, discarding vegetables. Add remaining carrots, leeks, celery, and parsley to kettle, and simmer until vegetables are tender. Add mushrooms and white onions and simmer another 20 minutes or until vegetables are tender.

Cut chicken into serving pieces and place in wide, deep bowls. Arrange some vegetables and ½ cup of rice in each bowl; ladle hot soup over all. Serve immediately. Serves 8, including 2 ozs. of chicken.

PER SERVING:
Cholesterol (mg): 60
Fat (grams): total 2; saturated less than 1

*Exchanges: milk 0; fruit 0; bread/starch 2;
vegetable 1; meat 2; fat 0*
Calories: 300

Soup à l'Oignon (French onion soup)

1 lb. onions
2 ozs. (¼ cup) margarine
  Salt and pepper to taste
½ teaspoon mustard
2 teaspoons plain flour
3¾ cups beef broth
¾ cup white wine
4–6 slices French bread, lightly toasted
½ cup Parmesan cheese, freshly grated

Peel and finely slice onions. Melt margarine in a large saucepan, then add onion rings, salt, pepper, and mustard. Cook over very gentle heat, stirring occasionally until onion is browned (20–30 minutes).

Add flour and stir until smooth. Add broth and white wine, stirring constantly, then bring to a boil and simmer 30 minutes. Taste and adjust seasoning.

Place slices of toasted bread on bottom of a soup tureen or in individual soup bowls, sprinkling with cheese. Pour hot soup carefully onto bread. Place under hot grill until cheese begins to brown. Serve immediately. Serves 4–6.

PER SERVING:
Cholesterol (mg): 5
Fat (grams): total 11; saturated 3
*Exchanges: milk 0; fruit 0; bread/starch 1;
vegetable 1; meat 0; fat 2*
Calories: 240

Basque Vegetable Soup

1½ cups dried white pea beans
2 large onions
5 large garlic cloves
1 medium turnip
4 carrots
4 medium-size potatoes
2 leeks
1 red bell pepper, whole
1 green bell pepper, whole
Bones and breast meat of roasting chicken, uncooked
2 teaspoons whole dried thyme
½ small cabbage head
1 cup red wine
Croutons for garnish

Soak dried pea beans overnight. Peel and chop onions, garlic, turnip, carrots, and potatoes. Wash and trim leeks and cut into 1-in. pieces. Discard seeds and pulp from peppers and cut into julienne strips

Place pea beans, onions, garlic, turnip, carrots, potatoes, leeks, green and red peppers, chicken bones and meat, and thyme in a large soup kettle; add water to cover. Bring to a boil and cook until vegetables are tender.

Continue cooking 30 minutes more. Remove chicken bones and peppers and discard. Reserve meat.

Discard core and limp outer cabbage leaves; shred the rest. Cut chicken meat into julienne strips and add, with cabbage, to soup. Cook 10 to 15 minutes more, adding water if soup is too thick. Add wine and cook 15 minutes more.

Ladle soup into bowls and garnish with croutons. Serves 8.

PER SERVING:
Cholesterol (mg): 40
Fat (grams): total 3; saturated 1
Exchanges: milk 0; fruit 0; bread/starch 1;

vegetable 1; meat 2; fat 0
Calories: 230

Cream of Pea Soup

1½ lbs. quick-cooking dried split peas
3 quarts chicken broth
3 small carrots
2 small onions
3 tablespoons margarine
1 large leek
1½ teaspoons sugar
2 cups fresh green peas, cooked
1 13-oz. can evaporated skim milk
1 tablespoon margarine
Pepper, freshly ground to taste
Croutons for garnish

Rinse dried split peas, drain, and place in large soup kettle. Add 3 quarts chicken broth, bring to a boil, reduce heat, and simmer 10 minutes. Skim froth from top of soup.

Peel and grate carrots and onions. Melt margarine in a skillet. Saute grated vegetables until golden. Wash and chop leek and add to sauteed vegetables. Cook 10 minutes over low heat. Stir vegetable mixture and sugar together into broth. Simmer until split peas are tender, about 2 hours.

Rub fresh-cooked peas through a fine sieve. Force soup mixture through the same sieve. Return mixture to kettle and stir in evaporated skim milk. Heat, but do not boil, stirring occasionally. Just before serving, add margarine and sprinkle with pepper. Serve hot with a garnish of croutons. Serves 10.

PER SERVING:
Cholesterol (mg): 3
Fat (grams): total 9; saturated 1
Exchanges: milk 0; fruit 0; bread/starch 1;
vegetable 1; meat 1; fat 1
Calories: 240

Cabbage Soup

1 medium cabbage head
2 large onions
2 carrots
1 large potato, pared
3 cups skim milk
2 tablespoons low-fat yogurt
1 bay leaf
½ teaspoon dill weed
½ teaspoon rosemary
    Pepper, freshly ground to taste

Shred the cabbage. Thinly slice onions, carrots, and potato. Place vegetables in heavy saucepan with a small amount of water. Cover and cook slowly until tender.

Add milk, yogurt, bay leaf, dill weed, rosemary, and pepper. Continue to cook about 15 minutes longer. Serves 6.

PER SERVING:
Cholesterol (mg): 0
Fat (grams): total 0; saturated 0
Exchanges: milk 0; fruit 0; bread/starch 1;
vegetable 0; meat 0; fat 0
Calories: 81

Greek Lemon Soup

1 quart chicken broth
1 tablespoon cornstarch
¼ cup rice, uncooked
4 tablespoons fresh lemon juice
    Egg substitute equivalent to 3 eggs

Take one cup chicken broth and stir in cornstarch. After cornstarch has dissolved, pour into saucepan and add rest of chicken broth. Heat broth on medium heat, add rice, and cook until tender. Remove from heat.

Bring egg substitute to room temperature. Beat lemon juice into egg substitute. Whisk half the broth, a little at a time, into egg substitute mixture. Pour egg substitute mixture back into remaining broth, mixing well. Return to low heat and cook, stirring constantly, just until soup is thickened. Serves 4.

PER SERVING:
Cholesterol (mg): 1
Fat (grams): total 1; saturated 0
Exchanges: milk 0; fruit 0; bread/starch 0;
vegetable 2; meat 1; fat 0
Calories: 112

Mushroom Soup

1 lb. mushrooms, finely chopped
4 tablespoons margarine
2 tablespoons flour
2 cups chicken broth
1 13-oz. can evaporated skim milk
    Pepper, freshly ground to taste

Saute mushrooms in margarine over low heat, stirring constantly; add flour; mix well. Slowly add chicken broth. Transfer to double boiler to keep warm. Just before serving, add evaporated skim milk and heat thoroughly. Stir in pepper before serving. Serves 4–6.

PER SERVING:
Cholesterol (mg): 3
Fat (grams): total 9; saturated 2
Exchanges: milk 1; fruit 0; bread/starch 0;
vegetable 0; meat 0; fat 2
Calories: 162

✳ Spinach Soup

3 tablespoons olive oil
1 cup water
1 large leek, sliced thin
1 carrot, peeled and sliced
1 celery stalk, sliced
6 cups chicken broth
6 large bunches fresh spinach, stems removed
½ cup Parmesan cheese, freshly grated
  Croutons

In large kettle, add olive oil, water, leek, carrot, and celery. Cook until very soft. Add chicken broth and bring to boil. Add spinach. Cook 2 minutes uncovered until spinach wilts. Transfer to food processor in small batches. Puree until very smooth. Transfer to large bowl. Serve garnished with grated cheese and croutons.

This soup is best used immediately as the color will change if left standing. Serves 10–12.

PER SERVING:
Cholesterol (mg): 4
Fat (grams): total 7; saturated 2
Exchanges: milk 0; fruit 0; bread/starch 0;
vegetable 1; meat 1; fat 0
Calories: 124

✳ Spanish Gazpacho

1 quart tomato juice
  Juice of 1 lemon
2 medium green bell peppers, finely chopped
½ cup scallions with tops, chopped
½ cup celery, chopped
1 zucchini, finely chopped

1 small cucumber, seeded, finely chopped
3 cloves garlic, minced
2 tablespoons olive oil
1 teaspoon basil
   Tabasco to taste

In large bowl, combine tomato and lemon juices; mix well. Add remaining ingredients. Mix well and chill. If thinner consistency is desired, add cold water. Serves 6.

PER SERVING:
Cholesterol (mg): 0
Fat (grams): total 5; saturated less than 1
Exchanges: milk 0; fruit 0; bread/starch 0;
vegetable 2; meat 0; fat 1
Calories: 87

Egg Drop Soup

2 13¾-oz. cans chicken broth
1 tablespoon cornstarch
2 egg whites, beaten
2 tablespoons green onion, sliced

In medium saucepan, slowly stir chicken broth into cornstarch. Cook, stirring constantly, until slightly thickened. Slowly pour in well-beaten egg whites, and remove soup from heat. Add green onion. Serves 4.

PER SERVING:
Cholesterol (mg): less than 1
Fat (grams): total 1; saturated less than 1
Exchanges: milk 0; fruit 0; bread/starch 0;
vegetable 0; meat 1; fat 0
Calories: 52

Broccoli Bisque

1 cup onion, minced
3 stalks celery
½ cup leek, thinly sliced
2 cloves garlic, minced
2 tablespoons margarine
1½ lbs. broccoli, trimmed
3 cups chicken broth
1 12-oz. can evaporated skim milk
¼ teaspoon dry mustard
1 teaspoon Spike
Pepper to taste

In large covered kettle, saute onion, celery, leek, and garlic in margarine until tender. Remove florets from broccoli and reserve. Slice stalks. Add slices and chicken broth to kettle; simmer 15 minutes; remove from heat. Puree mixture in food processor or blender. Return to kettle and stir in evaporated skim milk and broccoli florets. Add seasonings. Simmer 10 minutes. Serve hot or cold. Serves 6.

PER SERVING:
Cholesterol (mg): 3
Fat (grams): total 5; saturated 1
Exchanges: milk 0; fruit 0; bread/starch 1;
vegetable 0; meat 1; fat 0
Calories: 140

Vichyssoise

2 medium-size onions
6 leeks
6 tablespoons margarine
5 medium-size potatoes*
1¼ quarts chicken broth
2 cups skim milk
2 13-oz. cans evaporated skim milk
   Pepper, freshly ground to taste
   Chives, minced

Peel and chop onions. Slice leeks, using only white part. Heat margarine in a soup kettle, and add chopped onions and leeks. Saute until onions are golden and transparent. Peel and slice potatoes very thin. Add potatoes, together with chicken broth, to soup kettle. Place over medium heat and cook until potatoes are tender.

Whirl mixture in an electric blender until smooth. Place in refrigerator; when well chilled, add skim milk and evaporated skim milk. Add pepper to taste. Place icy-cold soup in chilled bowls and sprinkle with minced chives. Serve at once. Serves 8.

*Note: You can make a mock Vichyssoise by substituting cauliflower for potatoes. It tastes delicious and has fewer calories.

PER SERVING:
Cholesterol (mg): 4
Fat (grams): total 2; saturated 2
Exchanges: milk 1; fruit 0; bread/starch 1;
vegetable 2; meat 0; fat 0
Calories: 267

✳
Confetti Soup

2 carrots, sliced
1 cup leek or green onions, sliced
1 10-oz. pkg. frozen broccoli, chopped
1 10-oz. pkg. frozen cauliflower
1½ cups chicken broth
3 cups skim milk
1 tablespoon cornstarch
1 teaspoon Spike
  Pepper, freshly ground to taste

In large saucepan, cook carrots and leek or onions until almost tender. Add broccoli, cauliflower, and chicken broth. Continue to cook until vegetables are tender. In a blender, blend half the vegetables until smooth and return to saucepan. Combine ½ cup skim milk with cornstarch; add to vegetable mixture in saucepan. Stir in remaining milk and Spike. Cook and stir 1–2 minutes more. Remove from heat and add pepper. Serves 8.

PER SERVING:
Cholesterol (mg): 0
Fat (grams): total 0; saturated 0
Exchanges: milk 1; fruit 0; bread/starch 0;
vegetable 0; meat 0; fat 0
Calories: 80

✳
Italian Bean Soup

1 cup dried navy beans
2 quarts water
1 cup onion, chopped
1 cup green bell pepper, chopped
1 cup carrots, chopped
½ cup celery, chopped
1 teaspoon dried basil
1 teaspoon oregano
1 teaspoon vegetable-flavored bouillon
   granules
¼ teaspoon dry mustard
2 cloves garlic, minced
3 8-oz. cans tomato sauce
½ cup whole-wheat elbow macaroni, uncooked
1 15-oz. can garbanzo beans

Sort and wash beans; place in Dutch oven. Cover with water 2 in. above beans; bring to a boil and cook over high heat 3 minutes. Remove from heat; cover and let stand 1 hour. Drain beans; add 2 quarts water and next 10 ingredients. Cover and simmer 1½ hours or until beans are tender, stirring occasionally. Add macaroni and garbanzo beans and cook about 15 minutes or until macaroni is tender. Makes about 3½ quarts, or 14 one-cup servings.

PER SERVING (one cup):
Cholesterol (mg): 0
Fat (grams): total 0; saturated 0
Exchanges: milk 0; fruit 0; bread/starch 1;
vegetable 0; meat 0; fat 0
Calories: 104

Seafood Pasta Soup

½ lb. small pasta shells
2 tablespoons olive oil
½ cup onion, diced
½ cup green bell pepper, diced
½ cup red or yellow bell pepper, diced
½ teaspoon garlic, minced
½ lb. mushrooms, sliced
1 14-oz. can Italian plum tomatoes, chopped
2 cups chicken broth
½ cup white wine
1 lb. sea scallops, halved if large
¼ cup parsley, chopped
Pepper, freshly ground to taste
½ cup Parmesan cheese, freshly grated

Cook pasta according to package directions. Drain, toss with 1 tablespoon olive oil. Reserve. Heat remaining oil over medium heat in large Dutch oven. Add onion, peppers, garlic, and mushrooms. Cook until peppers are just crisp-tender and mushrooms are soft, about 5 minutes. Add tomatoes, broth, and wine. Heat to boil. Add scallops, parsley, pepper, and reserved pasta. Cover and return to boil. Remove from heat. Let stand 5 minutes. To serve, ladle soup into bowls and sprinkle with Parmesan cheese. Serves 8.

PER SERVING:
Cholesterol (mg): 34
Fat (grams): total 6; saturated 2
Exchanges: milk 0; fruit 0; bread/starch 1;
vegetable 1; meat 2; fat 0
Calories: 260

Fresh Tomato Soup
I like to make this when tomatoes are at their peak

2¼ lbs. fresh tomatoes
1 tablespoon vegetable oil
4 scallions, chopped
4 cloves garlic, minced
2½ cups chicken broth
4 tablespoons fresh basil
1 bay leaf
2 teaspoons sugar
½ cup white wine
2 cups fresh tomatoes, chopped
1 tablespoon parsley

Place tomatoes (a few at a time) in large pot of boiling water. Leave in about 30 seconds. Remove and slip off skins. Quarter tomatoes and remove seeds. Put tomatoes in blender and blend 1 minute.

Heat oil in large saucepan, and saute chopped scallions until transparent. Add garlic and tomatoes. Lower heat and simmer 5 minutes. Stir in chicken broth, herbs, and sugar. Cover pan and simmer 30 minutes. Add wine and chopped tomatoes and cook another 15 minutes. Remove from heat and stir in parsley. Serves 4–6.

PER SERVING:
Cholesterol (mg): less than 1
Fat (grams): total 4; saturated less than 1
Exchanges: milk 0; fruit 0; bread/starch 1;
vegetable 1; meat 0; fat 1
Calories: 155

Vegetarian Minestrone

3 tablespoons olive oil
2 cloves garlic
½ cup onion, chopped
3 large carrots, cut into ½-in. slices
2 medium potatoes, diced
1 medium leek, thinly sliced
3 stalks celery
1 cup fresh parsley, tightly packed
⅔ cup cannellini (white lima beans), picked over
    and rinsed, soaked in water overnight, drained
1 14-oz. can Italian plum tomatoes
6 cups water
1 15-oz. can chick peas
½ cup small elbow macaroni
2 zucchini, cut into ½-in. slices
2 cups shredded cabbage, loosely packed
1 tablespoon oregano
1 tablespoon basil
1 cup red wine
8 teaspoons Parmesan cheese, freshly grated

In large soup pot, heat olive oil. Saute garlic and onion until onion becomes limp, about 3 minutes. Add carrots, potatoes, leek, celery, ½ the parsley, cannellini beans, and plum tomatoes with their juice plus 6 cups of water. Bring to boil, cover, and reduce heat. Simmer until cannellini beans are soft, about 1 hour.

Add chick peas, macaroni, and zucchini. Cook uncovered over medium heat 5 minutes, adding water if soup becomes too thick. Add cabbage, oregano, basil, and red wine. Cook about 5 additional minutes. Ladle soup into bowls and top with 1 teaspoon Parmesan cheese and remaining parsley. Serves 8–10.

PER SERVING:
Cholesterol (mg): *less than 1*

Fat (grams): total 6; saturated less than 1
Exchanges: milk 0; fruit 0; bread/starch 2;
vegetable 0; meat 0; fat 1
Calories: 205

✳
Chinese Hot Pot

4 13¾-oz. cans chicken broth
1 cup white wine
¼ cup Tamari soy sauce
2 tablespoons sugar
2 3½-oz. pkgs. oriental-style noodles (without
   flavor packets)
8 ozs. oriental-style vegetables, such as
   mushrooms, carrots, broccoli
1 jar baby corn
1 lb. chicken breasts, boneless, skinned, cut
   into bite-size pieces
1 bunch watercress, trimmed
4 green onions, cut into 1-in. lengths
1 cup fresh pea pods

Combine broth, wine, soy, and sugar in 5-quart skillet or stove-top casserole. Break noodles in half; add to skillet with vegetables, corn, and chicken. Bring to boil. Reduce heat to medium-low; cook 3 minutes. Remove pan from heat. Stir in watercress, onions, and pea pods. Serve immediately. Serves 8.

PER SERVING:
Cholesterol (mg): 42
Fat (grams): total 4; saturated less than 1
Exchanges: milk 0; fruit 0; bread/starch 2;
vegetable 1; meat 2; fat 0
Calories: 293

Japanese Mushroom Soup with Noodles

1 oz. dried mushrooms
½ small onion
1 clove garlic
1½ lbs. fresh mushrooms, minced
2 tablespoons margarine
¼ teaspoon thyme
4 cups chicken broth
1 cup dry white wine
¼ lb. no-yolk noodles
½ lb. snow peas
½ cup radishes, sliced
1 tablespoon red-wine vinegar
Pepper, freshly ground to taste
2 teaspoons parsley, chopped

Pour 3 cups boiling water over dried mushrooms and let stand at least 2 hours. Take softened mushrooms from liquid and reserve liquid. In a food processor, mince dried mushrooms, onion, garlic, and about ¾ of the fresh mushrooms.

Melt 1 tablespoon margarine in a soup pot, add minced mushroom mixture, and cook over medium-high heat about 1 minute. Add second tablespoon margarine and continue cooking about 2 more minutes. Add thyme, chicken broth, wine, and mushroom liquid to pot and bring to a boil. Lower heat and simmer 30 minutes.

Strain mushroom broth and discard vegetables. Bring broth back to a simmer. Add noodles and cook about 12 minutes or until tender. Add remainder of mushrooms, snow peas, and radishes to broth and cook about 2 minutes. Stir in vinegar and cook 1 more minute. Remove from heat and stir in pepper and parsley. Serves 6.

PER SERVING:
Cholesterol (mg): less than 1
Fat (grams): total 5; saturated less than 1

Exchanges: milk 0; fruit 0; bread/starch 1;
vegetable 1; meat 0; fat 1
Calories: 207

Parsley Soup

2 potatoes, peeled and cut up
2 onions, chopped
1 tablespoon margarine
1 10¾-oz. can condensed chicken broth
1 cup parsley, fresh snipped
½ teaspoon Spike
   Worcestershire sauce, dash
   White pepper to taste
2 12-oz. cans evaporated skim milk

Cook potatoes, onions, and margarine in ¾ cup water until tender. Add broth, parsley, Spike, and Worcestershire; season with white pepper if desired. Transfer to blender container; blend until smooth. Return to saucepan and add milk; heat through. Serves 4.

PER SERVING:
Cholesterol (mg): 6
Fat (grams): total 4; saturated 0
Exchanges: milk 0; fruit 0; bread/starch 2;
vegetable 0; meat 1; fat 1
Calories: 235

*

Spicy Oatmeal Soup

1 tablespoon margarine
1 tablespoon peanut oil
2 large leeks, cleaned and thinly sliced (about
   2½ cups)*
4 carrots, peeled and cut into ½-in. slices
2 medium potatoes, diced
2 medium zucchini, sliced
2 celery stalks, thinly sliced
6 cups chicken broth
1 tablespoon dried chives
1 tablespoon dried shallots
½ tablespoon tarragon
½ tablespoon basil
1 tablespoon Spike
2 drops hot sauce, or to taste
½ cup quick-cooking oatmeal
1 cup white wine

Heat margarine and peanut oil in large saucepan and add leeks. Cook 2–3 minutes over medium to high heat. Add carrots, potatoes, zucchini, celery, and chicken broth. Bring to a boil. Add chives, shallots, tarragon, basil, Spike, and hot sauce. Boil gently 20 minutes. Add oatmeal and cook another 5 minutes. Add wine and cook another 15 minutes.

*Note: You can substitute green onions if leeks are not available.

PER SERVING:
Cholesterol (mg): less than 1
Fat (grams): total 5; saturated less than 1
Exchanges: milk 0; fruit 0; bread/starch 1;
vegetable 0; meat 0; fat 1
Calories: 153

Salads and Salad Dressings

A meal is not complete without a salad. We are fortunate to live in a country where even exotic and tropical fruits and vegetables are available and can be enjoyed. Every meal cries out for a salad accompaniment. Just think, no dish is as versatile as the salad. It can be appetizer, main dish, side dish, or dessert.

For those wishing to lower their cholesterol intake, adding salad to the diet can be a big help; edibles from the Plant Kingdom contain zero cholesterol. In addition, salad adds color and freshness to your meals. Nearly every type of food, including seafood, poultry, and meat, can form the basis of a delicious salad. So don't limit yourself to thinking of salad as "rabbit food."

Many salads can be satisfying, nutritious main dishes. Salads can be warm or cold, crunchy or soft, tossed or molded. They can be dressed with a sweet dressing or a pungent one. They can be sprinkled with herbs or topped with fruit. Let your imagination be your guideline and your creativity your inspiration.

You will find recipes in this chapter for vegetable, seafood, poultry, meat, fish, rice, and pasta as well as old-fashioned fruit salads. Many of them are heirlooms but all will satisfy your family and friends. Turn over a new leaf—literally—and reward your family and friends with better health deliciously. In addition to salads, this chapter also features dressings that will make your salads the center of attention.

✳
Italian Salad Dressing

1 cup olive oil
¼ cup lemon juice
¼ cup tarragon vinegar
1 teaspoon salt
1 teaspoon sugar
¼ teaspoon dry mustard
¼ teaspoon paprika
⅛ teaspoon thyme, ground
2 cloves garlic, crushed

Shake all ingredients in tightly covered jar. Refrigerate at least 2 hours. Makes 1½ cups of dressing.

PER SERVING (one tablespoon):
Cholesterol (mg): 0
Fat (grams): total 9; saturated 1
Exchanges: milk 0; fruit 0; bread/starch 0;
vegetable 0; meat 0; fat 2
Calories: 80

✳
French Dressing

½ cup olive oil
½ cup vegetable oil
½ cup catsup (low-sodium)
½ cup vinegar (tarragon, wine, or cider is best)
¼ cup sugar
2 tablespoons chives, minced
2 tablespoons parsley, minced
2 tablespoons onion, minced
1 garlic clove, crushed
1 tablespoon lemon juice
1 teaspoon dry mustard
¼ teaspoon paprika
   Salt, dash
   Pepper, dash

Shake all ingredients in tightly covered jar. Refrigerate at least 3 hours.

PER SERVING (two tablespoons):
Cholesterol (mg): 0
Fat (grams): total 27; saturated 4
Exchanges: milk 0; fruit 0; bread/starch 0;
vegetable 2; meat 0; fat 5
Calories: 280

✳
Soy-Garlic Dressing

3 tablespoons light soy sauce
3 tablespoons vegetable oil
2 cloves garlic, crushed
½ teaspoon sugar
¼ teaspoon ginger
   Pepper, dash

Shake all ingredients in tightly covered jar. Refrigerate. Makes about ⅓ cup dressing, or five tablespoons.

PER SERVING (one tablespoon):
Cholesterol (mg): 0
Fat (grams): total 8; saturated 1
Exchanges: milk 0; fruit 0; bread/starch 0;
vegetable 0; meat 0; fat 2
Calories: 82

✳
Creamy Oil Dressing

2 tablespoons vegetable oil
1 tablespoon white wine vinegar
1 tablespoon light mayonnaise
¼ teaspoon dry mustard
1 teaspoon lemon juice
⅛ teaspoon Burst O'Lemon

Shake all ingredients in tightly covered jar. Makes about ¼ cup dressing, or four tablespoons.

PER SERVING (one tablespoon):
Cholesterol (mg): 0
Fat (grams): total 5; saturated less than 1
Exchanges: milk 0; fruit 0; bread/starch 0;
vegetable 0; meat 0; fat 1
Calories: 41

Vinaigrette Dressing

½ cup olive oil
2 tablespoons red wine vinegar
1 teaspoon celery salt
1 teaspoon dry mustard
1 clove garlic, finely chopped
   Salt, dash
   Pepper, dash

Shake all ingredients in tightly covered jar. Makes about ⅓ cup dressing, or five tablespoons.

PER SERVING (one tablespoon):
Cholesterol (mg): 0
Fat (grams): total 22; saturated 3
Exchanges: milk 0; fruit 0; bread/starch 0;
vegetable 0; meat 0; fat 4
Calories: 192 per teaspoon

Asparagus Vinaigrette

   1 teaspoon sugar
1½ teaspoons salt
   ⅛ teaspoon pepper
   ¼ teaspoon paprika
      Garlic juice, few drops
   ⅓ cup vinegar
   1 cup olive oil
   3 tablespoons green onion, chopped
   2 tablespoons parsley, chopped
   2 tablespoons pimiento, chopped
   1 tablespoon capers
   2 large cans asparagus, drained

Combine sugar, salt, pepper, paprika, and garlic juice. Add vinegar and olive oil slowly, beating thoroughly. Add onion, parsley, pimiento, and capers to oil mixture. Pour vinaigrette sauce over asparagus. Marinate in refrigerator overnight or longer. Serves 6.

PER SERVING:
Cholesterol (mg): 0
Fat (grams): total 36; saturated 6
Exchanges: milk 0; fruit 0; bread/starch 0;
vegetable 1; meat 0; fat 7
Calories: 338

Spinach Salad with Poppy Seed Dressing

¾ cup sugar
⅓ cup white vinegar
1 cup vegetable oil
1 teaspoon dry mustard
1 teaspoon dried shallots
2 tablespoons poppy seeds
1 lb. fresh spinach, stems removed, cut into
   bite-size pieces
½ lb. fresh mushrooms, sliced thin

Combine sugar, vinegar, oil, dry mustard, shallots, and poppy seeds in a tight-fitting jar. Shake to blend. Refrigerate. Makes 1½ cups dressing.

When ready to serve, place spinach and mushrooms in a bowl. Stir dressing and pour over salad. Toss well. Serves 8.

PER SERVING:
Cholesterol (mg): 0
Fat (grams): total 28; saturated 4
Exchanges: milk 0; fruit 0; bread/starch 0;
vegetable 4; meat 0; fat 5
Calories: 346

Blueberry Bavarian Salad

SALAD

1½ cups hot water
1 pkg. black raspberry gelatin
½ pkg. lemon gelatin
1 can blueberry pie filling
Grated rind of 1 lemon
2 teaspoons lemon juice
2 tablespoons sugar

TOPPING

1 cup mock sour cream
2 tablespoons sugar
2 teaspoons lemon rind, grated

Salad: Mix hot water and gelatins; stir until dissolved. Cool until syrupy; add pie filling, grated lemon rind, lemon juice, and sugar. Pour into a mold or individual molds; chill until firm. Serves 6–8.

Topping: Combine all ingredients; mix well. Serve over salad.

PER SERVING:
Cholesterol (mg): 0
Fat (grams): total 0; saturated 0
Exchanges: milk 0; fruit 4; bread/starch 0;
vegetable 0; meat 0; fat 0
Calories: 258

✳

West Coast Salad

¼ cup plus 3 tablespoons raspberry-flavored
  vinegar, divided
1 tablespoon vegetable oil
1½ teaspoons water
1 tablespoon honey
2½ cups water
4 4-oz. chicken breast halves, boned and skinned
½ lb. fresh spinach
1 cup fresh raspberries
½ cup fresh mushrooms, sliced
1 cup alfalfa sprouts

Combine 3 tablespoons vinegar, oil, water, and honey
in a jar. Cover tightly and shake vigorously. Chill.

Bring 2½ cups water and remaining ¼ cup vinegar to
a boil in a large, non-aluminum skillet. Add chicken; cover,
reduce heat, and simmer 10 minutes or until chicken is
done. Drain. Cut chicken into cubes.

Remove stems from spinach; wash leaves thoroughly
and pat dry on paper towels. Gently rinse raspberries;
drain. Arrange chicken and raspberries evenly among 4
spinach-lined plates. Carefully ring plate with mushrooms
and place one or two slices among raspberries. Drizzle with
dressing. Top salad with alfalfa sprouts. Serves 4.

PER SERVING:
Cholesterol (mg): 73
Fat (grams): total 7; saturated 2
Exchanges: milk 0; fruit 0; bread/starch 1;
vegetable 0; meat 3; fat 0
Calories: 251

Parsley and Garbanzo Bean Salad
Eat as a salad or use as a filling in a pita bread sandwich

4 cups fresh parsley, chopped
2 15½-oz. cans garbanzo beans
1 large green bell pepper, chopped
½ cup green onions, chopped
1 large tomato, seeded and diced
¼ cup fresh lemon juice
1 garlic clove, minced
   Salt and pepper to taste
½ cup olive oil

Combine parsley, beans, green pepper, onions, and tomatoes. Blend lemon juice, garlic, salt, and pepper together in another bowl and whisk in olive oil in a thin stream. Toss well with salad. Serves 12.

PER SERVING:
Cholesterol (mg): 0
Fat (grams): total 11; saturated 1
Exchanges: milk 0; fruit 0; bread/starch 2;
vegetable 0; meat 0; fat 2
Calories: 251

Cranberry Cream Salad
A very tasty salad for the holidays

1 3-oz. pkg. cherry gelatin
1 cup hot water
1 1-lb. can whole cranberry sauce
½ cup celery, diced
¼ cup golden raisins
1 cup Mock Sour Cream (pg. 214)

Dissolve gelatin in hot water. Chill until slightly thickened. Fold cranberry sauce into gelatin with celery and raisins. Fold in mock sour cream. Pour mixture into a 1-quart mold. Chill until firm. Serves 4–6.

PER SERVING:
Cholesterol (mg): 0
Fat (grams): total 0; saturated 0
Exchanges: milk 0; fruit 3; bread/starch 0; vegetable 0; meat 0; fat 0
Calories: 170

Rotini Salad

1 recipe Italian Salad Dressing (pg. 66)
8 ozs. rotini
2 cans white tuna
2 medium tomatoes, chopped
1 cup mushrooms, sliced
1 small jar marinated artichoke hearts
¼ cup green bell pepper, sliced
¼ cup radishes, sliced
¼ cup part-skim mozzarella cheese, shredded
¼ cup black olives, sliced

Cook rotini, drain. Combine with remaining ingredients. Pour dressing over salad. Chill. May be made without tuna. Serves 6.

PER SERVING:
Cholesterol (mg): 47
Fat (grams): total 6; saturated 2
Exchanges: milk 0; fruit 0; bread/starch 1; vegetable 2; meat 3; fat 0
Calories: 280

Baked Seafood Salad

1 small green bell pepper, chopped
1 small onion, chopped
1 cup celery, chopped
1 lb. imitation crab meat
1 lb. small scallops, cooked
1 cup mock sour cream
1 teaspoon Spike
1 teaspoon Worcestershire sauce
1 cup breadcrumbs
2 tablespoons margarine

Mix all ingredients except breadcrumbs and margarine in casserole. Sprinkle breadcrumbs on top; dot with margarine. Bake 30 minutes at 350°. Do not overbake. Serves 6.

PER SERVING:
Cholesterol (mg): 35
Fat (grams): total 6; saturated 0
Exchanges: milk 0; fruit 0; bread/starch 1; vegetable 0; meat 3; fat 0
Calories: 255

Crunchy Broccoli Salad

2 lbs. fresh broccoli
½ lb. fresh mushrooms, sliced
½ cup mock sour cream
½ cup light mayonnaise
1 teaspoon sugar
⅛ teaspoon pepper
1 teaspoon grated onion
1 garlic clove, crushed
1 8-oz. can water chestnuts, drained and sliced

Cut off and discard tough ends of broccoli stalks. Break florets into small clusters. Reserve stems for another use. Steam broccoli for about 10 minutes or until tender-crisp. In a small bowl, combine mushrooms, mock sour cream, mayonnaise, sugar, pepper, onion, and garlic. In a large salad bowl, combine cooked broccoli and water chestnuts. Add creamed mixture; toss lightly. Cover and refrigerate 2 hours or more to blend flavors. Serves 4.

PER SERVING:
Cholesterol (mg): less than 1
Fat (grams): total 5; saturated less than 1
Exchanges: milk 0; fruit 0; bread/starch 1;
vegetable 3; meat 0; fat 0
Calories: 198

Award Winning Macaroni Salad

8 oz. small elbow macaroni, uncooked
1 cup whipped low-fat cottage cheese
¼ cup low-fat yogurt
2 tablespoons vinegar
2 teaspoons prepared mustard
1 teaspoon sugar
1 tablespoon lemon juice
¼ teaspoon celery seed
¼ teaspoon oregano
  Pepper, freshly ground to taste
1 pkg. frozen peas, thawed
½ cup celery, diced
¼ cup green onions, chopped

Cook macaroni according to package directions; drain. Pour cold water over macaroni; let stand while preparing salad. In a small bowl, combine cottage cheese, yogurt, vinegar, mustard, sugar, lemon juice, celery seed, oregano, and pepper. In a large salad bowl, combine cooked macaroni, peas, celery, and onion. Pour dressing over macaroni; toss to blend. Serve immediately or cover and refrigerate until ready to serve. Serves 6.

PER SERVING:
Cholesterol (mg): 2
Fat (grams): total 2; saturated less than 1
Exchanges: milk 0; fruit 0; bread/starch 3;
vegetable 0; meat 0; fat 0
Calories: 227

✳
Golden Gate Salad

½ cup whipped low-fat cottage cheese
¼ cup low-fat yogurt
1 tablespoon lemon juice
¼ teaspoon Dijon mustard
1 tablespoon fresh parsley, chopped
1 teaspoon dried tarragon, crumbled
    Pepper, freshly ground to taste
3 cups cooked chicken, diced
    Lettuce leaves
1 cup seedless grapes, cut in half
2 tomatoes, cut in quarters
1 cucumber, cut into 8 sticks

In a medium bowl, combine cottage cheese, yogurt, lemon juice, mustard, parsley, tarragon, and pepper; stir in chicken. Cover and refrigerate 2–3 hours to blend flavors. To serve, arrange lettuce leaves on 4 individual plates. Add grapes to chicken salad and spoon chicken mixture onto lettuce leaf. Garnish each salad with tomatoes and cucumbers. Serves 4.

PER SERVING:
Cholesterol (mg): 180
Fat (grams): total 6; saturated 2
Exchanges: milk 0; fruit 1; bread/starch 0;
vegetable 0; meat 5; fat 0
Calories: 350

✳
Chinese Coleslaw

1 small head cabbage, shredded
½ cup white vinegar
⅓ cup sugar
1 teaspoon coarse salt
¼ teaspoon pepper, freshly ground

½ **cup radishes, sliced**
2 **teaspoons dried shallots**

Put cabbage into a bowl. In a jar with tight-fitting lid, combine vinegar, sugar, salt, pepper, radishes, and shallots. Shake well to blend. Pour dressing over cabbage and mix well. Refrigerate. Serves 4.

PER SERVING:
Cholesterol (mg): 0
Fat (grams): total 0; saturated 0
Exchanges: milk 0; fruit 0; bread/starch 0;
vegetable 3; meat 0; fat 0
Calories: 80

Divine Cucumber Salad

6 **medium or 3 large cucumbers, peeled and**
   thinly sliced
1 **large red onion, sliced and separated into rings**
½ **cup white vinegar**
3 **tablespoons sugar**
1 **teaspoon coarse salt**
¼ **teaspoon pepper, freshly ground**
¼ **teaspoon ginger, ground**
1 **tablespoon chives, fresh or freeze-dried**
   Oregano, dash

Layer cucumbers in a bowl. Add onions. In a jar with a tight-fitting lid, combine vinegar, sugar, salt, pepper, ginger, chives, and oregano. Shake well. Pour dressing over cucumbers and refrigerate. Serves 4–6.

PER SERVING:
Cholesterol (mg): 0
Fat (grams): total less than 1; saturated 0
Exchanges: milk 0; fruit 0; bread/starch 0;
vegetable 4; meat 0; fat 0
Calories: 104

Mandarin Beets with Citrus Dressing

BEETS
  1 recipe Citrus Dressing (below)
  2 bunches beets, cooked, cooled, and thinly sliced
  2 red onions, thinly sliced
  1 11-oz. can mandarin orange segments, drained

CITRUS DRESSING
  ¼ cup vegetable oil
  2 tablespoons fruit-only orange marmalade*
  2 tablespoons lemon juice
  ¾ teaspoon salt
    Pepper, dash

Beets: Place beets, onions, and mandarin orange segments in a bowl. Pour dressing over salad and toss well. Serves 6.
  Dressing: Shake all ingredients in tightly covered jar. Makes about ½ cup of dressing, enough for 6 servings.
  *Note: See Brand Index.

PER SERVING:
Cholesterol (mg): 0
Fat (grams): total 9; saturated 1
Exchanges: milk 0; fruit 0; bread/starch 1;
vegetable 0; meat 0; fat 2
Calories: 170

Sombreros (Taco Salad)

1 lb. lean beef, ground
1½ lbs. turkey, ground
2 tablespoons olive oil
8 ozs. mild taco sauce
1 head iceberg lettuce, shredded
10 scallions, chopped
1 pt. cherry tomatoes, halved
6 ozs. taco cheese, shredded
8 tostadas
Parsley sprigs (optional)

Brown ground beef and turkey in olive oil. Drain well. Mix with taco sauce. In a large salad bowl, arrange lettuce. Layer scallions, tomatoes, and cheese on top of lettuce. Add beef and turkey mixture. Place one tostada on each plate and mound the meat mixture on top. Garnish with sprig of parsley if desired. Serves 8.

PER SERVING:
Cholesterol (mg): 77
Fat (grams): total 18; saturated 6
Exchanges: milk 0; fruit 0; bread/starch 0;
vegetable 2; meat 3; fat 2
Calories: 313

La Poet Potato Salad

    4 lbs. new potatoes
    12 scallions, chopped
    10 tablespoons fresh parsley, chopped
    1 cup mock sour cream
    3 hard-boiled eggs, yolks removed
       Dill sprigs

Cook potatoes until just done. Peel and slice. In a large bowl, combine potatoes with scallions, parsley, and mock sour cream. Garnish with chopped hard-boiled egg whites and dill. Serves 8–12.

PER SERVING:
Cholesterol (mg): 0
Fat (grams): total 0; saturated 0
Exchanges: milk 0; fruit 0; bread/starch 2;
vegetable 1; meat 0; fat 0
Calories: 174

Basque Tomatoes
This dish is not only beautiful but easily portable.
Serve when tomatoes are at their peak

    8 firm ripe tomatoes
    ½ cup parsley, chopped
    1 clove garlic, minced
    1 teaspoon salt
    1 teaspoon sugar
    ¼ teaspoon pepper
    ½ cup black olives (optional)
    ¼ cup olive oil
    2 tablespoons tarragon vinegar
    1 teaspoon Dijon mustard

Slice tomatoes and spread them in a shallow dish. Sprinkle with parsley. Combine remaining ingredients, mix

well, and pour over tomatoes. Cover and refrigerate. May
be made 2 days ahead. Serves 8.

PER SERVING:
Cholesterol (mg): 0
Fat (grams): total 10; saturated 1
Exchanges: milk 0; fruit 0; bread/starch 0;
vegetable 2; meat 0; fat 2
Calories: 133

Brown Rice and Chicken Salad

2 cups brown rice, uncooked
2 cups water
2 cups chicken, cooked and diced
12 scallions, thinly sliced
2 celery ribs, chopped
2 medium green bell peppers, chopped
½ cup black olives, sliced
¼ cup pimiento, minced
½ pt. cherry tomatoes
½ cup parsley, chopped
½ cup radishes, sliced
¼ cup olive oil
¼ cup white wine vinegar

In a covered saucepan, cook rice in water until liquid
is absorbed and rice is fluffy, approximately 25 minutes.
Remove from heat and cool. Add remaining ingredients
and toss.

Imitation crab meat or tuna can be added instead of
chicken. Serves 8.

PER SERVING:
Cholesterol (mg): 60
Fat (grams): total 12; saturated 2
Exchanges: milk 0; fruit 0; bread/starch 1;
vegetable 0; meat 2; fat 1
Calories: 262

Salade Nicoise with Dressing
A classic bistro dish found in Paris

SALAD
- 2 lbs. green beans, cut in 1½-in. lengths
- 2 green bell peppers, cut in thin rounds
- 2 cups celery, sliced
- 1 pt. cherry tomatoes
- 5 medium red potatoes, cooked and sliced (with skins left on)
- 21 ozs. canned tuna, drained
- 10 large black olives, pitted
- 1 large red onion, thinly sliced
- 2 tablespoons fresh basil, chopped; or 1 tablespoon dried basil
- ⅓ cup parsley, finely chopped
- ¼ cup scallions, finely chopped

DRESSING NICOISE
- 2 teaspoons Dijon mustard
- 2 tablespoons wine vinegar
- 6 tablespoons olive oil
- 2 cloves garlic, minced
- 1 teaspoon fresh thyme; or ½ teaspoon dried thyme
- Pepper, freshly ground to taste

Salad: Steam beans until tender-crisp, about 15 minutes. Drain and rinse under cold water. Place beans, green peppers, celery, tomatoes, and potatoes in a large salad bowl, arranging in a symmetrical pattern. Flake tuna over vegetables. Scatter olives and red onions over all. Sprinkle with basil, parsley, and scallions. Toss with dressing after bowl has been presented. Serves 8–10.

Dressing: Shake all dressing ingredients in a tightly covered jar and refrigerate 1 hour.

PER SERVING:
Cholesterol (mg): 20
Fat (grams): total 11; saturated 2

*Exchanges: milk 0; fruit 0; bread/starch 0;
vegetable 4; meat 2; fat 1
Calories: 261*

Court Salad with Raspberry Vinaigrette

This is an elegant salad to serve at your formal dinner parties or for a luncheon

SALAD

1 bunch watercress, washed and torn into bite-size pieces
2 heads Bibb lettuce, torn into bite-size pieces
1 lb. mushrooms, sliced
1 15-oz. can artichoke hearts
1 bunch white radishes, sliced
½ cup raspberry vinaigrette (recipe below)
1 cup raspberries

RASPBERRY VINAIGRETTE

¼ cup raspberry vinegar
½ teaspoon salt
1 cup olive oil
½ teaspoon Dijon mustard
½ teaspoon pepper, freshly ground

Place greens, mushrooms, artichoke hearts, and radishes in a large bowl. Shake Vinaigrette ingredients together and drizzle over salad, then toss. Serve with berries on top of each mound of greens. Serves 10, including dressing.

*PER SERVING:
Cholesterol (mg): 0
Fat (grams): total 12; saturated 1
Exchanges: milk 0; fruit 0; bread/starch 0;
vegetable 3; meat 0; fat 2
Calories: 181*

Seafood Pasta Salad with Divine Cream Dressing

PASTA
> 1 lb. pasta shells
> ⅓ cup olive oil
> ¼ cup white wine vinegar
> 1 tablespoon sherry wine vinegar
> Pepper, freshly ground to taste

Cook pasta *al dente* (slightly underdone). Drain, rinse in cold water, and place in a large bowl. Mix with oil and vinegars. Season to taste with pepper. Cover and refrigerate. You can keep this 2 days in the refrigerator.

VEGETABLES
> 12 thin asparagus spears (fresh if possible), trimmed and cut into 1½-in. lengths
> 2½ cups broccoli florets, in bite-size pieces
> 2½ cups peas, fresh or frozen
> 10 scallions
> 1 pt. cherry tomatoes
> 2 large heads romaine lettuce, torn into bite-size pieces

Separately boil or steam asparagus and broccoli until tender-crisp, about 15 minutes. Steam fresh peas briefly or use defrosted uncooked frozen peas. Mince scallions; combine with tomatoes. If you are not making the salad to be served now, store vegetables in separate plastic bags in the refrigerator. These can be prepared up to 2 days in advance.

SEAFOOD
> 2 lbs. bay scallops or halved sea scallops
> 2 lbs. imitation crab meat, cut into 2-in. lengths
> ⅓ cup olive oil
> 3 tablespoons white wine vinegar
> 3 tablespoons red wine vinegar

1 clove garlic, minced
2 scallions, minced
    Pepper, freshly ground to taste
1 teaspoon Spike

Poach scallops in simmering water until opaque, about 2 minutes. Drain. Combine scallops and crab meat in a bowl. Add oil, vinegars, and garlic; mix well. Reserve minced scallions, Spike, and pepper for salad assembly.

DIVINE CREAM DRESSING
    ⅓ cup white wine vinegar
    2 tablespoons Dijon mustard
    ½ cup packed fresh basil leaves; or 4
        tablespoons dried basil, crushed
    2 cloves garlic
    ⅓ cup vegetable oil
    1 cup mock sour cream
    ½ cup skim milk
    3 tablespoons parsley, minced
    ¼ cup chives, snipped

In food processor or blender, combine vinegar, mustard, basil, and garlic. Add oil slowly and process until smooth. Add mock sour cream, skim milk, parsley, and chives. Process until smooth.

To assemble: Arrange romaine as a border on large platter. Toss pasta with vegetables and tomato-scallion mixture. Place in center of platter and make a well in center of pasta. Drain seafood; toss with minced scallions, pepper, and Spike. Mound in center of pasta. Serve with Divine Cream Dressing. Serves 10.

PER SERVING:
Cholesterol (mg): 42
Fat (grams): total 24; saturated 3
Exchanges: milk 0; fruit 0; bread/starch 4;
vegetable 0; meat 3; fat 3
Calories: 600

Tomato Aspic

Perfect for a picnic on the 4th of July; serve in small individual molds, which can be decorated to fit the mood

1 recipe Mock Sour Cream (pg. 214)
1 envelope unflavored gelatin
2 cups tomato juice or V8 juice
1 tablespoon lemon juice
2 teaspoons vinegar
   Red pepper sauce, dash
½ cup celery, chopped
¼ cup cucumber, chopped
¼ cup black olives, chopped
   Bibb lettuce

Sprinkle gelatin on ½ cup of tomato juice in saucepan to soften; stir over low heat until gelatin is dissolved. Stir into remaining tomato juice; stir in lemon juice, vinegar, and pepper sauce. Refrigerate until slightly thickened, about 25 minutes. Stir celery, cucumber, and olives into gelatin mixture; pour into individual molds. Refrigerate until firm, at least 3 hours. Unmold on lettuce, top with Mock Sour Cream, and garnish with parsley. Serves 4.

PER SERVING:
Cholesterol (mg): 1
Fat (grams): total 3; saturated 0
Exchanges: milk 0; fruit 0; bread/starch 0;
vegetable 2; meat 0; fat 1
Calories: 92

Tomatoes Stuffed with Beans

This combination salad and vegetable dish is a nice accompaniment to any meat dish and can also be used with an omelette brunch recipe

1 recipe Italian Dressing (pg. 66)
1 9-oz. pkg. frozen Italian green beans
½ cup mushrooms, sliced
½ cup green onion, sliced
¼ cup green bell pepper, diced
¼ cup black olives, sliced
6 medium tomatoes
½ teaspoon basil leaves for garnish

Prepare Italian green beans according to package directions; drain thoroughly. Place in bowl with mushrooms, onions, green pepper, and olives. Pour on dressing and refrigerate 2 hours, tossing occasionally.

Meanwhile, cut thin slice from tops of 6 medium tomatoes. Scoop out center, leaving shell about ¼-in. thick. Invert on paper towels to drain; chill. Before serving, season shells with a touch of basil and fill with bean mixture. Garnish with basil leaves. Serves 6.

PER SERVING:
Cholesterol (mg): 0
Fat (grams): total 12; saturated 0
Exchanges: milk 0; fruit 0; bread/starch 0;
vegetable 3; meat 0; fat 2
Calories: 160

Tomato and Cucumber Salad with Basil

1 recipe Vinaigrette Dressing (pg. 69)
2 heads red leaf lettuce, torn into bite-size pieces
4 large tomatoes, cut into wedges
3 cucumbers, sliced but not peeled
½ cup scallions, cut into ½-in. pieces
6 fresh basil leaves, snipped
⅓ cup Roquefort cheese, crumbled

Combine lettuce, tomatoes, cucumbers, scallions, and basil in large bowl. Toss with dressing. Sprinkle with cheese. Serves 8.

PER SERVING:
Cholesterol (mg): 8
Fat (grams): total 26; saturated less than 1
Exchanges: milk 0; fruit 0; bread/starch 0;
vegetable 4; meat 0; fat 5
Calories: 334

Italian Mushroom Salad

½ cup olive oil
2 tablespoons tarragon vinegar
2 tablespoons lemon juice
½ teaspoon dried basil leaves
¼ teaspoon dry mustard
1 clove garlic, crushed
½ lb. mushrooms, sliced
   Boston lettuce leaves
¼ cup black olives, sliced
¼ cup parsley, snipped

Shake first 6 ingredients in tightly covered jar; pour over mushrooms. Cover and refrigerate no longer than

2 hours. Arrange lettuce leaves on 4 plates. Drain mushrooms and place on top of lettuce leaves. Garnish with black olives and parsley. Serves 4.

PER SERVING:
Cholesterol (mg): 0
Fat (grams): total 30; saturated 4
Exchanges: milk 0; fruit 0; bread/starch 0;
vegetable 1; meat 0; fat 6
Calories: 285

South-of-the-Border Bean Salad

> 1 recipe French Dressing (pg. 67) or Creamy
> Oil Dressing (pg. 68)
> 1 16-oz. can whole green beans, drained
> 1 15-oz. can garbanzo beans, drained
> 1 15-oz. can kidney beans, drained
> 1 12-oz. can whole kernel corn with sweet pep-
> pers, drained
> 1 medium onion, thinly sliced and separated
> into rings
> ½ cup taco cheese, shredded
> 8 lettuce cups

Toss beans, corn, and onion with dressing. Refrigerate at least 1 hour. Before serving, toss with cheese and spoon into lettuce cups. Serves 8, with one tablespoon of dressing per serving.

PER SERVING:
Cholesterol (mg): 7
Fat (grams): total 16; saturated 4
Exchanges: milk 0; fruit 0; bread/starch 2;
vegetable 0; meat 1; fat 2
Calories: 329

Asparagus Salad Supreme with Dijon Dressing

SALAD

Dijon Mustard Dressing (below)

1 15½-oz. can artichoke hearts

1 15-oz. can white asparagus, drained and cut

1 15-oz. can green asparagus, drained and cut

1 cup mushrooms, sliced

Romaine lettuce leaves

½ cup celery, chopped

¼ cup pimiento, diced

½ cup black olives, sliced

DIJON MUSTARD DRESSING

½ cup olive oil

1 clove garlic, crushed

¼ cup lemon juice

2 tablespoons parsley

1 teaspoon capers

1 tablespoon Dijon-style mustard

Salt, dash

Pepper, dash

Prepare Dijon Mustard Dressing by shaking all ingredients in a tightly covered jar and refrigerate. Makes about ¾ cup.

At least 2 hours before serving, place artichoke hearts, asparagus, and mushrooms in a bowl and pour dressing over them. Cover and refrigerate at least 2 hours. Remove vegetables with slotted spoon; reserve Dijon Mustard Dressing. Arrange vegetables on lettuce. Garnish with celery, pimiento, and black olives. Serve with reserved Dijon Mustard Dressing. Serves 8, including dressing.

PER SERVING:

Cholesterol (mg): 0

Fat (grams): total 5; saturated 2

Exchanges: milk 0; fruit 0; bread/starch 0; vegetable 1; meat 0; fat 1
Calories: 75

Salade Provençale

2 large heads romaine lettuce, torn into bite-size pieces
1 small head Boston lettuce, torn into bite-size pieces
2 6½-oz. jars marinated artichoke hearts
3 scallions, cut into 1-in. pieces
6 radishes, sliced
½ red bell pepper, chopped
½ yellow bell pepper, chopped
½ cup black olives, sliced
1 large tomato, sliced and quartered
1 recipe Soy-Garlic Dressing (pg. 68)

Place lettuce in bowl and add remaining ingredients. Pour dressing over salad and toss well. Serves 12.

PER SERVING:
Cholesterol (mg): 0
Fat (grams): total 5; saturated 0
Exchanges: milk 0; fruit 0; bread/starch 0; vegetable 2; meat 0; fat 1
Calories: 80

Terrific Caesar Salad

Garlic Croutons
Coddled Egg

Prepare Garlic Croutons and Coddled Egg. See directions below.

DRESSING
1 clove garlic, cut into halves
4 anchovy fillets, cut up
⅓ cup olive oil
1 teaspoon Worcestershire sauce
½ teaspoon salt
¼ teaspoon dry mustard
Pepper, freshly ground

Place garlic, anchovy fillets, olive oil, Worcestershire sauce, salt, dry mustard, and pepper into a cruet. Shake well and refrigerate.

SALAD:
1 large bunch romaine lettuce, torn into bite-
size pieces
⅓ cup fresh Parmesan cheese, grated
1 tablespoon fresh lemon juice

To assemble salad: Place romaine in alad bowl and toss with dressing. Sprinkle cheese over top and toss again. Pour Coddled Egg on top and add lemon juice. Toss well. Sprinkle Croutons over top of salad and toss again. Serves 6.

GARLIC CROUTONS (Baked)
Heat oven to 400°. Trim crusts from 4 slices of white bread. (Day old bread is best for this.) Spread both sides of bread with margarine and sprinkle with garlic powder. Cut into ½-in. cubes. Bake on ungreased baking pan or cookie sheet, stirring occasionally until golden brown and crisp, 10 to 15 minutes.

GARLIC CROUTONS (Sauteed)
Trim crusts from 4 slices of white bread. (Day old bread is best for this.) Spread both sides of bread with mar-

garine and sprinkle with garlic powder. Cut into ½-in. cubes. Place a frying pan on medium-high heat and add 3 tablespoons olive oil. Saute lightly until golden brown. Remove from pan and drain on paper towel.

CODDLED EGG

Separate egg and discard yolk. Place enough water in a saucepan to produce a depth of about 3 in. Bring to boiling. Remove from heat and place egg white in a cup or poached egg cup and place it in the water for about 1 minute. Remove from hot water to prevent further cooking.

PER SERVING:
Cholesterol (mg): 2
Fat (grams): total 18; saturated 3
Exchanges: milk 0; fruit 0; bread/starch 0;
vegetable 2; meat 0; fat 3
Calories: 218

Raspberry Mold

3 small pkgs. raspberry gelatin
2 cups boiling water
3 10-oz. pkgs. frozen raspberries, partially thawed
3 cartons low-fat yogurt (total about 16 oz.)

Dissolve gelatin in boiling water. Stir in raspberries until gelatin thickens and raspberries thaw. Stir yogurt into gelatin mixture. Spoon into a 12-cup mold. Chill until firm. Serves 12–14.

For a smaller portion, cut recipe in third.

PER SERVING:
Cholesterol (mg): less than 1
Fat (grams): total 0; saturated 0
Exchanges: milk 0; fruit 3; bread/starch 0;
vegetable 0; meat 0; fat 0
Calories: 195

Antipasto Salad with Garlic Dressing

This salad is pretty hardy, but to turn it into a main dish salad, just add pasta shells, bows, or tortellini

SALAD

1 recipe Garlic Dressing (below)
1 15½-oz. can garbanzo beans, drained
1 jar (about 6½ ozs.) marinated artichoke hearts
½ cup roasted red peppers
¼ cup black olives, pitted, drained, and sliced
2 bunches romaine, torn into bite-size pieces
1 bunch red leaf lettuce, torn into bite-size pieces
½ cup low-fat salami, sliced
½ cup part-skim mozzarella cheese
¼ cup Parmesan cheese, freshly grated

GARLIC DRESSING

2 tablespoons olive oil
1 tablespoon plus 1½ teaspoons tarragon vinegar
¼ teaspoon prepared mustard
¼ teaspoon Worcestershire sauce
1 clove garlic, crushed
Pepper, dash

Salad: Place beans, artichoke hearts, roasted peppers, and olives in salad bowl; add lettuce. Pour salad dressing over all and toss well. Arrange salami on salad greens. Sprinkle both cheeses over top. Serves 8.

Dressing: Shake all ingredients in tightly covered jar. Makes about ¼ cup dressing.

PER SERVING:
Cholesterol (mg): 10
Fat (grams): total 9; saturated 2
Exchanges: milk 0; fruit 0; bread/starch 0;
vegetable 3; meat 0; fat 2
Calories: 166

Tropical Fruit Boats
with Banana Dressing

2 pineapples, cut in half
1 cup strawberries
1 medium banana, sliced
1 cup blueberries
1 cup watermelon balls
1 cup cantaloupe balls
2 kiwi fruits, peeled and sliced
½ cup low-fat cottage cheese
1 medium banana, cut up
2–3 tablespoons pineapple juice
1 tablespoon honey
2 tablespoons orange peel, grated

Run a serrated knife around the perimeter of each pineapple half and remove pineapple meat, leaving a ¼-in. shell. Place pineapple meat in a bowl. Add strawberries, banana, blueberries, watermelon, cantaloupe, and kiwi fruit; toss well to mix.

To make dressing, place cottage cheese, banana, pineapple juice, and honey in a blender; blend until smooth. Spoon fruit into pineapple halves. Top with 2 tablespoons dressing. Sprinkle grated orange peel on top. Serves 4.

PER SERVING:
Cholesterol (mg): 0
Fat (grams): total 0; saturated 0
Exchanges: milk 0; fruit 4; bread/starch 0; vegetable 0; meat 0; fat 0
Calories: 246

Summer Fruit Salad Bowl

1 kiwi, peeled and chopped
1 pt. strawberries, hulled and cleaned
1 apple, chopped
2 peaches, peeled and chopped
1 pear, peeled and chopped
1 pt. blueberries, rinsed well
1 fresh pineapple, peeled and chopped
½ cup seedless grapes, halved
2 tablespoons sugar
3 tablespoons Triple Sec

Combine fruit, sugar, and Triple Sec in a bowl and toss well. Can be chilled or served at room temperature. Serves 6.

PER SERVING:
Cholesterol (mg): 0
Fat (grams): total 0; saturated 0
Exchanges: milk 0; fruit 2½; bread/starch 0;
vegetable 0; meat 0; fat 0
Calories: 164

Waldorf Salad

2 medium Delicious apples, chopped
2 stalks celery, chopped
⅓ cup walnuts, coarsely chopped
½ cup golden raisins
½ cup Mock Sour Cream (pg. 214)
1 tablespoon honey
4–6 lettuce cups
Apple slices

Mix chopped apples, celery, walnuts, and raisins with mock sour cream. Add honey and stir to blend. Spoon salad into lettuce cups. Garnish with apple slices. Serves 4–6.

PER SERVING:
Cholesterol (mg): less than 1
Fat (grams): total 6; saturated less than 1
Exchanges: milk 0; fruit 2; bread/starch 0;
vegetable 0; meat 0; fat 1
Calories: 151

Fruit with Raspberry Dressing

½ **cup low-fat cottage cheese**
⅔ **cup raspberries**
2–3 **tablespoons skim milk**
1 **tablespoon honey**
½ **teaspoon poppy seeds**
1 **medium banana, sliced**
1 **cup strawberries, sliced**
1 **cup raspberries, whole**
1 **cup blueberries**
6 **lettuce leaves**

To make dressing, combine cottage cheese, raspberries, milk, honey, and poppy seeds in a blender. Cover and blend till smooth. In a medium bowl, combine banana, strawberries, raspberries, and blueberries. Toss to mix. Spoon fruit onto individual lettuce-lined plates. Top each serving of fruit with 2 tablespoons dressing. Serves 6.

PER SERVING:
Cholesterol (mg): 0
Fat (grams): total 0; saturated 0
Exchanges: milk 0; fruit 1; bread/starch 0;
vegetable 0; meat 0; fat 0
Calories: 76

Elegant Fruit and Cheese Ring

1 6-oz. pkg. lemon-flavored gelatin
2 cups boiling water
1 cup dry white wine
1 cup plain low-fat yogurt
1 cup strawberries, sliced
1 cup blueberries
½ cup part-skim mozzarella cheese (2 ozs., shredded)
Lettuce leaves

Dissolve gelatin in boiling water; stir in wine. Gradually beat gelatin mixture with yogurt. Chill until partially set (consistency of unbeaten egg whites). Fold in fruit and cheese. Turn mixture into a 5½ or 6-cup mold. Chill gelatin several hours or overnight until firm. Unmold onto lettuce leaves. Serves 8.

PER SERVING:
Cholesterol (mg): less than 1
Fat (grams): total 1; saturated less than 1
Exchanges: milk 0; fruit 1; bread/starch 0;
vegetable 0; meat 1; fat 0
Calories: 132

Summer Salad

¼ cup honey
1 tablespoon lemon juice
½ teaspoon orange peel, finely shredded
¼ teaspoon lemon peel, finely shredded
¼ teaspoon lime peel, finely shredded
¼ teaspoon cinnamon, ground
2 oranges, peeled and sliced crosswise
½ cup strawberries
1 cup blueberries

2 peaches, peeled and sliced
2 kiwi fruits, peeled and sliced

Combine honey, lemon juice, orange peel, lemon peel, lime peel, and cinnamon. Drizzle over orange slices in bowl; cover and chill for several hours or overnight. Chill remaining fruits. Drain oranges; reserve liquid. Arrange oranges in bottom of a bowl. Top with three layers of fruits. Pour reserved liquid over fruits. Serves 6.

PER SERVING:
Cholesterol (mg): 0
Exchanges: milk 0; fruit 2; bread/starch 0;
vegetable 0; meat 0; fat 0
Calories: 108

Pear and Grape Salad

Skim milk
1 cup low-fat cottage cheese, whipped
1 teaspoon sugar
2 large, ripe pears, halved and peeled
Lettuce
Seedless green grapes, halved
4 sprigs mint

Mix small amount of milk with cottage cheese and sugar; blend until spreading consistency. Place pear halves on lettuce leaves, cut side down; frost generously with cottage cheese. Press grapes, cut side down, onto pears, covering pears completely. Place a mint sprig where pear stem would be for color. Chill and serve on individual salad plates. Serves 4.

PER SERVING:
Cholesterol (mg): 3
Fat (grams): total less than 1; saturated 0
Exchanges: milk 0; fruit 1; bread/starch 0;
vegetable 0; meat 1; fat 0
Calories: 107

Oriental Chicken Salad

3½ tablespoons Tamari soy sauce
2 tablespoons vegetable oil
2 tablespoons balsamic vinegar
1 tablespoon sugar
1 clove garlic, minced
2 tablespoons chives, chopped
3 cups lettuce, torn
1½ cups cooked chicken, chopped
1 8-oz. can sliced water chestnuts
¼ cup green onions, diagonally sliced
1 pkg. pea pods, thawed
1 cup red cabbage, chopped
Chow mein noodles

In small bowl, whisk together first 6 dressing ingredients. Set aside. In large bowl, combine remaining salad ingredients except chow mein noodles. Just before serving, toss salad with dressing and top with chow mein noodles. Serves 6.

PER SERVING:
Cholesterol (mg): 0
Fat (grams): total 16; saturated 1
Exchanges: milk 0; fruit 0; bread/starch 2;
vegetable 0; meat 3; fat 1
Calories: 367

Meats

Meat is often the centerpiece of your meal. From a formal dinner to a backyard barbecue, your meat dish sets the tone and theme of the occasion. Americans enjoy a wide choice of meats regardless of the part of the country in which they are dining. Sunday dinner on the East Coast calls for roast beef; down South it might be ham; in the Midwest ribs are a favorite; in Texas a steak; and on the West Coast the barbecue is a favorite.

Meat consumption is the area of diet most critical to the success of any low-cholesterol program. It is true that to be successful, you will need to eliminate altogether some of the meats you may have eaten for years, such as ribs and 16-ounce steaks. I believe that you can make substitutions that will be every bit as tasty, and when you see what the changes have done to your cholesterol count, you won't miss the red meat at all.

Many families have developed favorite meat dishes that have been passed down from parent to child. The choices selected here are designed to be low in cholesterol and high in flavor. You can experiment and develop some favorites of your own, or modify recipes you have used for years.

On the pages that follow you will find some old favorites and some new recipes that use ground turkey instead of ground beef. Be sure to try them because I believe you will be very surprised at how good they are. Also included are some elegant recipes that will make your most formal dinner party memorable.

Veal with Mushroom-Dijon Sauce

SAUCE

¾ cup chicken broth
¾ cup dry white wine
1 small onion, chopped
3 tablespoons lemon juice
10 whole peppercorns
¼ cup chives, minced
2 tablespoons honey
2 teaspoons Dijon mustard
1½ cups fresh mushrooms, sliced
2 tablespoons water
2 teaspoons all-purpose flour
¼ cup fresh parsley, chopped
Lemon slices

VEAL

2 lbs. veal scallops
White pepper to taste
½ cup all-purpose flour
¼ cup olive oil
Juice of 1 lemon, freshly squeezed
½ cup dry white wine

Sauce: Combine chicken broth with the next five ingredients in a large pot. Bring mixture to a boil over
medium heat. Cover, reduce heat, and simmer 5 minutes.
Strain cooking liquid; discard onion, peppercorns, and
chives. Add honey, mustard, and mushrooms to chicken
broth; stir well. Bring to a boil and cook 10 minutes. Combine water and flour; stir well. Add to the broth; cook 1
minute or until slightly thickened, stirring constantly. Remove from heat, add parsley and lemon slices, and prepare veal.

Veal: Pound veal scallops until they are flat, and season with pepper. Flour the veal on one side only. Saute on
floured side in batches, using 2 tablespoons of olive oil for
each batch, until the veal turns white, about 45–60 seconds
over medium-high heat. Return all veal to the skillet, add
lemon juice and wine, and pour sauce over veal; heat
through. Arrange veal on a serving platter and pour sauce
over. Sprinkle with parsley. Serves 4.

PER SERVING:
Cholesterol (mg): 312
Fat (grams): total 24
Exchanges: milk 0; fruit 0; bread/starch 1;
vegetable 2; meat 7; fat 2
Calories: 594

Veal Chops and Mushrooms

3 tablespoons margarine
4 lean loin veal chops
1 medium onion, chopped
1 pound mushroom caps
1 8-oz. jar white onions
1 tablespoon flour
1 tablespoon tomato paste
¾ cup chicken broth
⅔ cup dry white wine
¼ cup dried shallots
¼ cup chives, minced
1 teaspoon tarragon
1 teaspoon basil
1 small bay leaf
¼ cup parsley, minced

In large heavy skillet, melt margarine. Brown veal chops quickly in skillet over high heat. Transfer chops to shallow casserole. In same skillet over medium heat, saute onions. Add remaining ingredients except parsley. Cover skillet and cook 5 minutes. Pour mixture over chops. Cover casserole. Bake in preheated 325° oven 1 hour. Sprinkle with parsley before serving. Serves 4.

PER SERVING:
Cholesterol (mg): 192
Fat (grams): total 9
Exchanges: milk 0; fruit 0; bread/starch 0;
vegetable 2; meat 4; fat 2
Calories: 357

Herb-Scented Leg of Lamb

1 5–6-lb. leg of lamb (do not have fell removed)
1 stick margarine, melted

6 cloves garlic
Garlic powder to taste
Oregano to taste
1½ tablespoons fresh mint

Place meat, skin-side down, on rack in open roasting pan. Pour margarine over roast. Cut several slits in surface of meat. In each slit insert 1 garlic clove. Sprinkle with garlic powder and oregano. Roast uncovered at 300° for about 1 hour. Add mint and return to oven for another 2–2½ hours or until meat thermometer registers 180° (allow 30–35 minutes per pound). Serves 12.

PER SERVING:
Cholesterol (mg): 29
Fat (grams): total 28
Exchanges: milk 0; fruit 0; bread/starch 0;
vegetable 0; meat 4; fat 4
Calories: 410

Oriental Lamb Chops

8 rib lamb chops
½ cup Tamari soy sauce
8 cloves garlic, minced

Marinate lamb chops in soy sauce for about ½ hour. Remove them from marinade and place on broiler pan. Pour marinade over the chops, and spoon minced garlic onto the chops. Broil chops 10–15 minutes on each side. Remove from broiler and serve. Serves 4.

PER SERVING:
Cholesterol (mg): 70
Fat (grams): total 37
Exchanges: milk 0; fruit 0; bread/starch 0;
vegetable 0; meat 3; fat 6
Calories: 434

Moussaka

1 small eggplant, peeled and cut into ¼-in.
slices
¼ lb. ground lamb or ground beef
½ lb. ground turkey
½ cup onion, chopped
½ green bell pepper, chopped
1 clove garlic, minced
½ cup tomato sauce
⅓ cup dry red wine
1 tablespoon parsley, chopped
Cinnamon, ground, dash
1 egg white, beaten
4 teaspoons all-purpose flour
Cinnamon, dash
Nutmeg, ground, dash
¾ cup skim milk
1 egg white, beaten
3 tablespoons Parmesan cheese, freshly grated

In saucepan, place eggplant slices in steamer basket over boiling water; cover and steam about 8 minutes. Drain on paper toweling and reserve.

In skillet, cook ground meat, onion, green pepper, and garlic until meat is browned; drain. Stir in tomato sauce, wine, parsley, dash cinnamon. Simmer, uncovered, 8 minutes. Remove from heat. Gradually stir half of the hot mixture into 1 beaten egg white; return to skillet.

To prepare sauce, in saucepan, combine flour, dash of cinnamon, and nutmeg and gradually stir in milk until smooth. Cook and stir until bubbly. Remove from heat. Gradually stir half of the hot sauce into 1 beaten egg white; return all to saucepan.

In 8x8x2-in. baking pan, place half the eggplant. Pour meat mixture over eggplant; top with remaining eggplant. Pour sauce over all. Sprinkle with Parmesan cheese. Bake in 325° oven about 30 minutes. Serves 4.

PER SERVING:
Cholesterol (mg): 55
Fat (grams): total 9; saturated 5
Exchanges: milk 0; fruit 0; bread/starch 0;
vegetable 1; meat 3; fat 1
Calories: 236

Light Beef Stroganoff

1 tablespoon margarine
3 tablespoons all-purpose flour
½ cup skim milk
¾ cup chicken broth
   Garlic powder, dash
¼ teaspoon pepper, freshly ground
1 tablespoon vegetable oil
1 clove garlic, minced
½ cup onion, chopped
¼ cup dried shallots
1½ lbs. lean round steak, sliced in thin strips
½ lb. fresh mushrooms, sliced
1 cup non-fat plain yogurt
¼ cup chives, minced

In a saucepan, melt margarine. Add 3 tablespoons flour. Cook, while mixing with a wire whisk, for about 1 minute. Add milk, chicken broth, garlic powder, and pepper. Continue stirring with wire whisk until mixture thickens and comes to a boil. Remove mixture from heat and set it aside.

Heat vegetable oil in large skillet. Add garlic, onion, shallots, and beef strips. Saute over medium heat until meat is browned. Add mushrooms, cover, and cook over low heat 10–15 minutes. Uncover; add sauce mixture and continue to cook until meat is tender. Add yogurt to mixture and cook until heated through. Top with chives. Serve over no-yolk noodles or rice. Serves 4.

PER SERVING:
Cholesterol (mg): 122
Fat (grams): total 24; saturated 9
Exchanges: milk 0; fruit 0; bread/starch 0; vegetable 2; meat 5; fat 3
Calories: 436

Beef and Mushroom Stir-Fry

12 ozs. beef, top round steak
½ cup cold water
3 tablespoons Tamari soy sauce
2 tablespoons dry red wine
4 teaspoons cornstarch
1 tablespoon cooking oil
8 ozs. fresh mushrooms, sliced
½ cup green onion, chopped
¼ cup celery, sliced diagonally
1 6-oz. pkg. frozen pea pods
1 small jar baby corn
½ cup water chestnuts, sliced

Cut beef into thin, bite-size strips. Combine water, soy sauce, wine, and cornstarch; set aside.

Preheat a wok or large skillet over high heat. Add 1 teaspoon of the oil. Stir-fry mushrooms and onions about 2 minutes or until crisp-tender; remove from wok.

Add remaining 2 teaspoons oil. Stir-fry half the beef at a time for about 2 minutes or until done. Return all beef to wok and push from center. Stir the soy mixture, and add it to center of wok. Cook and stir until thickened and bubbly. Remove from heat.

Add mushroom mixture, celery, pea pods, baby corn, and water chestnuts to wok. Stir to coat vegetables and meat with sauce. Serves 4.

You can cover with foil and freeze if desired. To reheat, remove foil and cover with vented, heavy-duty plastic wrap or waxed paper. Microwave 1 serving on 70% power (medium-high) for 5½–6½ minutes.

PER SERVING:
Cholesterol (mg): 60
Fat (grams): total 9; saturated 3
Exchanges: milk 0; fruit 0; bread/starch 1;
vegetable 2; meat 3; fat 3
Calories: 280

Boeuf a la Bourguignon
(Beef Burgundy)

1 cup beef bouillon
3 tablespoons all-purpose flour
1 tablespoon tomato paste
1 teaspoon meat glaze
   Vegetable cooking spray
2 lbs. lean beef, round or chuck
2 tablespoons sherry wine
1½ cups onion, chopped
1 cup Burgundy or other red wine
   Herb bouquet (sprig of parsley with 1 teaspoon each thyme, rosemary, tarragon in a cheesecloth bag)
12 medium-size mushrooms
¼ cup margarine
½ cup fresh parsley, chopped

Set out a large, heavy skillet with a tight-fitting cover. Put bouillon in a small bowl and blend to a paste with flour, tomato paste, and meat glaze. Set aside.

Wipe beef with a clean, damp cloth and cut into 3-in. pieces. Spray skillet with vegetable cooking spray and add meat. Brown on all sides. Remove from skillet and set aside.

Stir into skillet 2 tablespoons sherry wine. Add onions and cook until transparent, stirring occasionally. Blend in tomato paste mixture. Bring rapidly to boiling, stirring constantly. Stir in Burgundy wine and herb bouquet. Replace beef. Cover and simmer over low heat about 2½–3 hours or until meat is tender.

Clean and slice mushrooms. In a small skillet, combine margarine and mushrooms. Saute mushrooms until lightly browned. Add to meat. Complete cooking, remove and discard herb bouquet, and turn meat into a casserole dish. Sprinkle with parsley. Serves 4.

PER SERVING:
Cholesterol (mg): 120
Fat (grams): total 28; saturated 10
Exchanges: milk 0; fruit 0; bread/starch 1;
vegetable 0; meat 5; fat 2
Calories: 460

✳
Steak Da Vinci

1¼ lbs. lean, boneless beef round steak
   Vegetable cooking spray
1 cup onion, chopped
1 cup green bell pepper, chopped
1 clove garlic, minced
¼ cup dried shallots
1 14½-oz. can whole tomatoes, undrained and chopped
1 teaspoon beef-flavored bouillon granules

1 teaspoon oregano
½ teaspoon basil
1 teaspoon garlic powder
½ cup mushrooms, sliced
2 cups hot, cooked linguine
4 tablespoons Italian parsley, chopped
¼ cup Parmesan cheese, freshly grated

Trim any fat from steak and cut steak into 1-in. cubes. Spray a large non-stick skillet with cooking spray; place over medium-high heat until hot. Add steak and cook until browned. Remove from skillet; set aside.

Rinse skillet under hot water and dry. Spray again with cooking spray. Add onion, green pepper, garlic, and shallots to skillet and saute about 3 minutes or until tender. Return steak to skillet; add tomatoes and the next 4 ingredients, stirring well.

Cover meat mixture, reduce heat, and simmer about 30 minutes. Add mushrooms and simmer another 30 minutes. Uncover and cook mixture an additional 15 minutes or until meat is tender. Serve meat over linguine and sprinkle with parsley and cheese. Serves 4.

PER SERVING:
Cholesterol (mg): 84
Fat (grams): total 13; saturated 6
Exchanges: milk 0; fruit 0; bread/starch 2;
vegetable 3; meat 4; fat 6
Calories: 437

Very Special Beef Stew

Vegetable cooking spray

1¼ lbs. boneless beef round steak, cut into 1-in. cubes

1½ cups water

1 teaspoon Worcestershire sauce

2 bay leaves

1 clove garlic, minced

¼ teaspoon pepper

8 medium carrots, quartered

4 small potatoes, peeled and quartered

2 small zucchini, sliced

4 small onions, quartered

½ cup button mushrooms

1 tablespoon cornstarch

¼ cup cold water

½ cup red wine

Spray a Dutch oven with non-stick vegetable cooking spray. In Dutch oven, brown beef. Add water, Worcestershire, bay leaves, garlic, and pepper. Cook, covered, for 1¼ hours, stirring often. Remove bay leaves; add vegetables. Cover; cook 30 minutes. Drain, reserving liquid. Skim fat. Add water to liquid to make 1¼ cups; return to Dutch oven. Combine cornstarch and cold water; stir into liquid. Add wine. Cook and stir until bubbly; cook 2 minutes more. Add beef and vegetables; heat through. Serves 8.

PER SERVING:

Cholesterol (mg): 40

Fat (grams): total 6; saturated 3

Exchanges: milk 0; fruit 0; bread/starch 1; vegetable 1; meat 2; fat 0

Calories: 214

Stuffed Cabbage Leaves

12 large cabbage leaves
½ lb. ground meat and ½ lb. ground turkey; or
   1 lb. ground turkey
1 medium-size onion, minced
   Pepper, dash
½ cup rice, cooked
1 egg white, slightly beaten
1 cup tomato juice
2 tablespoons vinegar
3 tablespoons vegetable oil
¼ cup brown sugar
1 bay leaf

Wash cabbage leaves; steam in a colander over boiling water 5–10 minutes until they are pliant enough to roll. Remove from heat.

Mix meat, onion, pepper, rice, and egg. Trim hard center of each leaf, and place a spoonful of the meat filling on center of leaf. Fold sides up over filling, tucking in edges; or fasten with toothpick. Repeat until all leaves are filled. Place in a greased 2-quart baking dish.

Mix and pour over top, tomato juice, vinegar, and oil. Sprinkle brown sugar over top and add bay leaf. Bake covered, in a moderate 350° oven for 45 minutes, removing cover slightly before the end of baking to brown top. Additional liquid may be added during baking if needed. Serves 6.

PER SERVING:
Cholesterol (mg): 59
Fat (grams): total 15; saturated 4
Exchanges: milk 0; fruit 0; bread/starch 0;
vegetable 2; meat 3; fat 1
Calories: 260

✳
Sukiyaki

1 tablespoon margarine
1 lb. round steak, cut into very thin strips
1 cup mushrooms, sliced
1 5-oz. can bamboo shoots
2 stalks celery, thinly sliced diagonally
1 medium onion, sliced
5 green onions, cut into ¼-in. pieces
1½ cups soy sauce
1 cup sugar
½ cup sake or dry vermouth
2 cloves garlic, finely chopped
2 slices fresh ginger root, finely chopped
1 tablespoon sesame seed
2 tablespoons scallion tops, chopped
¼ lb. fresh spinach, stems removed and
  shredded

Heat a large skillet over low heat and add 1 tablespoon margarine. Add meat and brown on all sides over medium heat. When meat is browned, add the 5 vegetables, soy sauce, sugar, sake or vermouth, garlic, ginger root, and sesame seed.

Cover and bring to a boil; reduce heat to simmer, moving and turning mixture occasionally with a spoon, about 20 minutes or until vegetables are partially tender. Add scallion tops and spinach to the meat-vegetable mixture, partially cover skillet, and continue cooking 5–10 minutes. Serves 4.

PER SERVING:
Cholesterol (mg): 40
Fat (grams): total 10; saturated 3
Exchanges: milk 0; fruit 0; bread/starch 3;
vegetable 2; meat 3; fat 3
Calories: 450

All-American Meat Loaf

SAUCE
  1 cup tomato sauce
  1 cup barbecue sauce

MEAT LOAF
  2 lbs. lean ground beef
  1 tablespoon garlic powder
  ¼ teaspoon pepper, freshly ground
  ¼ teaspoon allspice, ground
  2 tablespoons Worcestershire sauce
1½ cups quick rolled oats
  1 can Campbell's zesty tomato soup
  ½ cup chili sauce
  ½ cup Mock Sour Cream (pg. 214)
  2 tablespoons dried onions
  2 egg whites, beaten
  ½ cup parsley, chopped
    Parsley sprigs

Sauce: In saucepan, combine sauce ingredients. Simmer uncovered for about 15 minutes. Remove from heat and set aside.

Meat Loaf: Combine meat with all remaining ingredients except parsley sprigs. Form into 8x4x3-in. loaf. Place loaf in greased 9x13-in. glass baking dish. Cover with heavy foil. Chill 1 hour. Remove from refrigerator and let come to room temperature.

Bake covered in preheated 350° oven 1 hour. Drain meat and use paper towels to absorb any remaining juices. Spoon sauce on top of meat loaf and bake uncovered 20–30 minutes or until loaf is glazed a dark brown. Turn off oven.

With door ajar, leave meat loaf in oven 10 minutes. Remove to platter and garnish with parsley. Serves 8.

PER SERVING:
Cholesterol (mg): 60
Fat (grams): total 10; saturated 4

Exchanges: milk 0; fruit 0; bread/starch 1; vegetable 1; meat 3; fat 0
Calories: 262

Deviled Dogs

4 turkey wieners, split lengthwise
4 hot dog buns
1 16-oz. can Heinz vegetarian beans
2 teaspoons prepared mustard
1 cup taco cheese
1 cup tomato, chopped
1 cup scallions, chopped
¼ cup jalapeño peppers, chopped

Place wieners in buns. Mix the remaining ingredients in a bowl. Place hot dogs in a square baking dish. Spoon bean mixture over wieners. Bake at 350° until warm, about 20 minutes. Serves 4.

Note: You can also grill the hot dogs on a barbecue grill and heat the beans and vegetables before spooning over the hot dogs.

PER SERVING:
Cholesterol (mg): 70
Fat (grams): total 21; saturated 9
Exchanges: milk 0; fruit 0; bread/starch 3; vegetable 0; meat 3; fat 2
Calories: 487

Turkey Burgers Deluxe

1 lb. ground turkey
½ cup oats
⅓ cup onions, chopped
1 egg white, beaten
1 teaspoon Tamari soy sauce

1 teaspoon Worcestershire sauce
1 teaspoon garlic powder
1 teaspoon dry mustard
2 tablespoons cracked pepper
½ cup fresh chives, minced
4 hamburger buns
4 onion slices
4 tomato slices

In a large bowl, combine all ingredients except buns, onion, and tomato slices. Mix well and shape meat mixture into 4 patties, each ½ in. thick. Broil burgers about 6 in. from heat. Serve burgers on buns with onion and tomato slices. Serves 4.

GREEK BURGERS

1 recipe Turkey Burgers Deluxe, above
2 pita breads, cut in half
1 cup tomato, chopped
½ cup cucumber, thinly sliced
6 tablespoons feta cheese, crumbled
½ cup onion, chopped

Prepare burgers and serve in pita bread halves with tomato, cucumber, feta cheese, and onions. Serves 4.

PER SERVING, Turkey Burgers:
Cholesterol (mg): 59
Fat (grams): total 12; saturated 3
Exchanges: milk 0; fruit 0; bread/starch 2;
vegetable 0; meat 3; fat 0
Calories: 335

PER SERVING, Greek Burgers without pita bread:
Cholesterol (mg): 78
Fat (grams): total 13; saturated 6
Exchanges: milk 0; fruit 0; bread/starch 1;
vegetable 0; meat 3; fat 1
Calories: 309

Loin of Pork in Wine Sauce

6 tablespoons olive oil
1 clove garlic, crushed
5 peppercorns, crushed
4 thick slices pork tenderloin; or 4 pork chops
¼ cup flour
    Pepper, freshly ground to taste
1 onion, finely chopped
¼ cup sweet red peppers, chopped
¼ cup beef broth
¼ cup dry white wine
1 tablespoon red wine vinegar
¼ cup chives, minced

Combine 4 tablespoons olive oil, garlic, and pepper-corns in a shallow pan. Add pork and turn pieces over to coat both sides. Cover with plastic wrap and marinate over-night, turning pork occasionally.

Heat remaining oil in a skillet. Dry pork with paper towels and dredge in flour and pepper. Fry on both sides until golden brown. Remove from pan. Add onion and red peppers and saute until softened. Add beef broth, wine, and vinegar and stir to scrape up any brown pieces cling-ing to bottom of pan.

Return pork to pan and simmer slowly, uncovered, 30 minutes, turning pork after 15 minutes. If sauce tends to stick, add 1 tablespoon of broth from time to time. Gar-nish with chives and serve with rice. Serves 4.

PER SERVING:
Cholesterol (mg): 93
Fat (grams): total 32; saturated 5
Exchanges: milk 0; fruit 0; bread/starch 0;
vegetable 2; meat 4; fat 4
Calories: 465

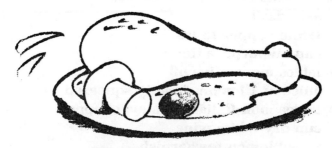

Poultry

When I was growing up, chicken on Sunday was a tradition and a vital part of most families' weekly menu. My grandmother must have known 150 different ways to prepare poultry, whose subtle taste allows the cook an unlimited choice of seasonings and sauces. Poultry can be baked, roasted, sauteed, poached, broiled, or stewed. It can be served hot or cold. It is very versatile and probably the favorite meat of most people. You can serve poultry with many interesting side dishes such as potatoes, pasta, or rice. Vegetables go well with poultry, and it stands on its own with no more than salad and bread.

You will enjoy these interesting dishes, featuring cornish hens, chicken, and turkey. I have continued the family tradition of chicken on Sunday, which pleases my husband, family, and friends. The meat is never a surprise, but everyone looks forward to an exciting preparation. If you always cook chicken the same way, try one of these recipes and I am confident you will get rave reviews.

✳

Chicken Limone

2 lbs. boneless chicken breasts*
Salt, dash
White pepper to taste
½ cup all-purpose flour
6 tablespoons olive oil
Juice of 1 lemon, freshly squeezed
1 tablespoon Italian parsley, chopped
½ cup dry white wine
Sliced lemon for garnish

Pound chicken until it is flat, then season with salt and pepper to taste. Flour chicken on one side only. Saute on floured side in batches, using 2 tablespoons olive oil for each batch, until chicken is cooked, about 20–25 minutes. Return chicken to skillet, add lemon juice, and sprinkle with parsley. Pour wine over chicken, turn heat up to high, and let wine bubble for about 2 minutes. Arrange chicken on individual, heated plates. Pour pan juices over chicken and garnish with a slice of lemon. Serves 4.

*Note: Veal is excellent in this recipe for a change.

PER SERVING:
Cholesterol (mg): 135
Fat (grams): total 25; saturated 5
Exchanges: milk 0; fruit 0; bread/starch 1;
vegetable 0; meat 6; fat 2
Calories: 513

*
Chicken Mousse

2 envelopes unflavored gelatin
2 cups chicken stock
1 lb. cooked chicken meat, shredded
5 tablespoons dry sherry
1 teaspoon dried leaf tarragon
½ cup green onions, chopped
   Pepper, freshly ground to taste
½ cup light mayonnaise
½ cup Mock Sour Cream (pg. 214)
2 teaspoons tomato paste
   To garnish: Watercress, black olives, and
   cherry tomatoes

Lightly grease a 5–6-cup mold with vegetable cooking spray. In a small saucepan, combine gelatin and ½ cup stock. Stir well; let stand 3 minutes. Stir over low heat until gelatin dissolves; cool slightly.

Combine remaining stock, gelatin mixture, and remaining ingredients in a blender or food processor fitted with the steel blade. Process until smooth. Pour into greased mold. Cover and refrigerate until set.

Run tip of a knife around edge of mold to loosen. Place a serving plate over mousse; invert mousse onto plate. Garnish with watercress, olives, and cherry tomatoes. Serves 6.

PER SERVING:
Cholesterol (mg): 81
Fat (grams): total 6; saturated less than 1
Exchanges: milk 0; fruit 0; bread/starch 0;
vegetable 0; meat 4; fat 0
Calories: 210

Chicken Cacciatore

1 chicken (3½-lb.), cut up and skinned
½ cup all-purpose flour
¼ cup olive oil
1 recipe Ultra Chic Marinara Sauce (pg. 213)
½ cup fresh Italian parsley, chopped

Roll chicken in flour. Saute in hot olive oil until golden brown. Place in roasting pan. Pour marinara sauce over chicken. Bake at 350° for 40 minutes or until tender. Place chicken in center of a platter and sprinkle with parsley. Surround with cooked spaghetti or rice. Pour all of the sauce over top. Serves 6.

PER SERVING:
Cholesterol (mg): 94
Fat (grams): total 23; saturated 5
Exchanges: milk 0; fruit 0; bread/starch 1;
vegetable 1; meat 5; fat 2
Calories: 460

Chicken and Vegetable Terrine

1 small green bell pepper
1 small red bell pepper
2 small carrots
1 zucchini
1 yellow squash
1½ lbs. boned and skinned chicken breasts,
    diced
1 clove garlic, crushed
½ teaspoon nutmeg, ground
2 tablespoons lemon juice
    Egg substitute equal to 3 eggs

1½ cups evaporated skim milk
½ cup mixed fresh herbs, such as basil, tarra-
gon, dill, and parsley

Wash peppers, carrots, zucchini, and yellow squash. Remove pepper seeds and pare vegetables as needed. Dice all vegetables and blanch lightly in boiling water. Drain and reserve.

In a food processor, puree chicken. Add garlic, nutmeg, and lemon juice. Process; then add egg substitute. Process again and add evaporated skim milk and chopped herbs. Mix well.

Pour chicken mixture into a bowl and chill slightly. Fold in blanched vegetables, then spoon mixture into a 4x8-in. loaf pan sprayed with vegetable cooking spray. Bake in a preheated 325° oven for 1–1½ hours or until terrine pulls away from sides of pan and is firm to the touch. Cool terrine, then chill overnight in refrigerator. To serve, cut into ½-in. slices. You can garnish each slice with a marinated artichoke heart. Serves 6.

PER SERVING:
Cholesterol (mg): 122
Fat (grams): total 4; saturated 1
Exchanges: milk 0; fruit 0; bread/starch 0;
vegetable 2; meat 4; fat 4
Calories: 270

Crispy Baked Chicken

1 frying chicken (2½–3 lbs.), cut into serving
   pieces
1 cup skim milk
1½ cups cornflake crumbs
1 tablespoon garlic powder
1 tablespoon oregano
1 tablespoon Spike

Remove all skin from the chicken; rinse and dry pieces thoroughly. Dip in milk, then roll in cornflake crumbs seasoned with garlic powder, oregano, and Spike. Let stand briefly so coating will adhere. Line a baking pan with aluminum foil and arrange chicken so none of the pieces touch. Bake at 400° for 45–60 minutes. The cornflake crumbs will form a crisp "skin." Serves 4.

PER SERVING:
Cholesterol (mg): 115
Fat (grams): total 7; saturated 2
Exchanges: milk 0; fruit 0; bread/starch 3;
vegetable 0; meat 3; fat 0
Calories: 405

Chicken Breasts and Balsamic Vinegar

4 skinless, boneless chicken breasts, about
   1½ lbs.
¾ lb. small mushrooms
2 tablespoons all-purpose flour
   Pepper, freshly ground to taste
3 tablespoons olive oil
6 cloves garlic, peeled

4 tablespoons balsamic vinegar
¾ cup chicken broth
1 bay leaf
¼ teaspoon dried thyme
¼ teaspoon dried tarragon
1 tablespoon margarine

Split each chicken breast lengthwise in half. Rinse mushrooms; drain and pat dry.

Season flour with pepper, and dredge chicken in mixture. Shake off excess flour.

Heat olive oil in a heavy skillet and cook chicken breasts until nicely browned on one side, about 4 minutes over moderately high heat. Add garlic. Turn chicken pieces and continue to cook chicken. Add mushrooms. Cook about 7 minutes; then add balsamic vinegar and broth. Add bay leaf, thyme, tarragon, and margarine. Cover closely and cook over moderately low heat 10 minutes, turning pieces occasionally.

Transfer chicken to a warm platter and set aside. Let sauce with mushrooms cook, uncovered, over moderately high heat about 6 minutes. Remove from heat. Discard bay leaf. Pour sauce over chicken and serve. Serves 4.

PER SERVING:
Cholesterol (mg): 101
Fat (grams): total 17; saturated 3
Exchanges: milk 0; fruit 0; bread/starch 0;
vegetable 1; meat 4; fat 2
Calories: 358

Stir-Fry Chicken with Broccoli

¼ cup Tamari soy sauce
1½ tablespoons dry sherry
¾ teaspoon ground ginger
1½ pounds boneless chicken breast in 1-in.
     pieces
  1 lb. broccoli, peeled
  7 tablespoons vegetable oil, divided
½ cup mushrooms
¼ cup pimiento, minced
½ cup celery
½ cup scallions, sliced
  1 large clove garlic, crushed

In a small bowl, combine soy sauce, sherry, ginger, and chicken. Let stand 10 minutes. Trim florets from broccoli and reserve. Cut tough ends from stalks and discard. Slice stalks diagonally into ¼-in. pieces. Steam florets and stalk slices 4–5 minutes until tender-crisp. Drain and rinse under cold water.

Heat 4 tablespoons oil in wok or large skillet. Add mushrooms, pimiento, celery, scallions, and garlic. Cook 4 minutes, stirring constantly. Transfer mixture to bowl. Heat remaining oil in wok. Add chicken mixture and broccoli. Stir fry 6 minutes or until chicken is opaque. Serve immediately. Serves 4–6.

PER SERVING:
Cholesterol (mg): 67
Fat (grams): total 18; saturated 3
Exchanges: milk 0; fruit 0; bread/starch 0;
vegetable 1; meat 4; fat 2
Calories: 317

Chicken and Leeks with Basil Cream Sauce

2 lbs. chicken breasts, boned
3 tablespoons margarine
1 pound leeks, cleaned and julienned
2 tablespoons shallots, chopped
½ cup cognac
1 cup dry white wine
3 cups chicken stock
2 cups evaporated skim milk
1 tomato, peeled, seeded, and diced
10 fresh basil leaves, chopped
　Salt, dash
　Pepper, freshly ground

Preheat oven to 400°. Melt margarine in a skillet over medium-high heat. Briefly saute chicken in batches without cooking through. Transfer chicken to a casserole, leaving margarine and pan juices in the skillet.

Bake chicken 15 minutes. Remove chicken from oven and set aside.

Saute julienne of leek in pan juices for 5 minutes and remove. Saute shallots until transparent. Remove and set aside. Add cognac to the pan, flame, and reduce to a syrup. Add white wine and reduce to a glaze. Add chicken stock and reduce to ¼ cup. Add evaporated skim milk and boil for 2 minutes. Add diced tomato, basil, leeks, and shallots. Season to taste with salt and pepper. Pour sauce over chicken and serve. Serves 6.

PER SERVING:
Cholesterol (mg): 93
Fat (grams): total 9; saturated 2
Exchanges: milk 0; fruit 0; bread/starch 1;
vegetable 1; meat 5; fat 1
Calories: 439

Chicken Marengo

1 frying chicken (about 3 lbs.), cut up and skinned
⅓ cup flour
   Salt and pepper, dash
¼ cup olive oil
1 clove garlic, crushed
3 tablespoons onion, chopped
4 tomatoes, quartered
1 cup white wine Herb bouquet (sprig of parsley and 1 teaspoon each thyme, rosemary,
   tarragon in cheesecloth bag)
2 tablespoons margarine
1 cup mushrooms, sliced
½ cup black olives, sliced
½ cup chicken broth
2 tablespoons cornstarch

Set out a large, heavy skillet with tight-fitting cover. Rinse and pat chicken dry. Shake chicken in a bag containing flour and a dash of salt and pepper. Heat oil and brown chicken in it. Add garlic and onions. Continue to cook on medium heat. Add tomatoes, wine, and herb bouquet. Cover and simmer over low heat about ½ hour.

In a small skillet, saute 2 tablespoons margarine and mushrooms. Add to chicken with olives.

To thicken, put chicken broth and cornstarch into a screw-top jar. Shake well. Remove chicken from skillet and discard herb bouquet. Gradually add broth-cornstarch liquid to mixture in skillet, stirring constantly. Boil 3–5 minutes until mixture thickens. Arrange chicken on a hot platter. Cover with the sauce. Serves 4.

PER SERVING:
Cholesterol (mg): 69
Fat (grams): total 15; saturated 2
Exchanges: milk 0; fruit 0; bread/starch 0;
vegetable 2; meat 4; fat 1
Calories: 311

Coq-au-Vin

6 tablespoons margarine
1 3½-lb. chicken, cut up and skinned
8 small onions or shallots
¼ cup brandy
1¼ cups red wine
1¼ cups chicken stock
  Pepper, freshly ground
  Bouquet garni
2 cloves garlic, crushed
½ lb. button mushrooms
¼ cup all-purpose flour
4 tablespoons fresh parsley, chopped

Melt 4 tablespoons of the margarine in a skillet and saute chicken until golden. Remove and drain. Peel onions, removing the rind. Fry onions in margarine until golden, stirring occasionally. Return chicken to the pan, pour in brandy, and ignite.

When flames have died down, add wine, chicken stock, pepper, bouquet garni, garlic, and mushrooms. Bring to boil, cover, and simmer gently for 35–45 minutes or until chicken is tender. Remove and discard bouquet garni. Remove chicken from pan and place the portions on a heated serving plate, keeping hot.

Mix remaining margarine with flour to a smooth paste (beurre manie). Bring cooking liquor in skillet to the boil and add the beurre manie in small pieces, stirring constantly. Add enough beurre manie to form a slightly thickened consistency. Allow the gravy to boil 2–3 minutes. Pour gravy over chicken, sprinkle with chopped parsley, and serve very hot. Serves 4.

PER SERVING:
Cholesterol (mg): 135
Fat (grams): total 23; saturated 5
Exchanges: milk 0; fruit 0; bread/starch 1;
vegetable 0; meat 6; fat 0
Calories: 455

Chicken Stew and Dumplings

1 chicken (2–3 lbs.), cut in serving pieces and
   skinned
Salt and pepper to taste
2 tablespoons margarine
½ cup water
1 cup onion, sliced
1 teaspoon Spike
1 can cream of chicken soup
1 soup can skim milk
1 10-oz. pkg. frozen mixed vegetables
1 cup Bisquick (no cholesterol) biscuit mix
⅓ cup skim milk

Sprinkle chicken with salt and pepper; brown in margarine in a large, heavy pan. Add water, onion, and Spike; cover. Simmer for 30 minutes. Stir in soup mixed with 1 soup-can quantity of skim milk; add mixed vegetables. Cover and bring to a boil. Simmer for 10 minutes, stirring occasionally. Combine biscuit mix and ⅓ cup skim milk; spoon onto stew. Cook for 10 minutes. Cover; cook 10 minutes longer. Serves 4.

PER SERVING:
Cholesterol (mg): 142
Fat (grams): total 18; saturated 4
Exchanges: milk 0; fruit 0; bread/starch 3;
vegetable 0; meat 6; fat 0
Calories: 570

Chicken Parmesan

4 split chicken breasts, skinned
¾ cup Parmesan cheese
6 tablespoons olive oil
1 clove garlic, minced
3 tablespoons flour
1½ cups chicken stock
½ cup sherry
1 cup mushroom caps
1 teaspoon each thyme and tarragon
2 tablespoons fresh parsley, chopped
1 lb. spaghetti, cooked

Dip chicken in cheese. Heat olive oil in heavy frypan; brown chicken until golden, turning to brown evenly. Remove from pan; place in casserole. Drain all but 3 tablespoons of oil from pan. Add garlic; cook until soft. Stir in flour until smooth. Add chicken stock, sherry, mushrooms, and spices. Cook, stirring until smooth and slightly thickened. Pour over chicken. Bake at 350° for 30–40 minutes. Sprinkle with parsley; serve with spaghetti. Serves 4.

PER SERVING:
Cholesterol (mg): 77
Fat (grams): total 8; saturated 3
Exchanges: milk 0; fruit 0; bread/starch 5;
vegetable 0; meat 4; fat 8
Calories: 600

*

Chicken Vesuvio

2 frying chickens (about 2½ lbs. each), cut up
and skinned
4 large red potatoes
¼ cup olive oil
¼ cup lemon juice, freshly squeezed
1 tablespoon fresh rosemary leaves
2 teaspoons garlic, minced
1 teaspoon Spike
¼ cup green onions, chopped
¼ cup black olives, sliced
1 cup mushrooms, sliced

Cut each chicken into 8 pieces. Rinse chicken pieces well and dry thoroughly. Scrub and quarter each potato without peeling. Place chicken and potatoes in a casserole. Season by drizzling olive oil and lemon juice over chicken and potatoes. Sprinkle on rosemary, garlic, and Spike. Marinate in the refrigerator for at least 30 minutes, turning occasionally.

Preheat oven to 425°. Remove chicken from refrigerator and add onion. Bake chicken for 30 minutes. Lower oven temperature to 400° and add olives and mushrooms. Cook another 30 minutes. Place chicken on platter and pour pan juices over all. Serves 4.

PER SERVING:
Cholesterol (mg): 15
Fat (grams): total 16; saturated 4
Exchanges: milk 0; fruit 0; bread/starch 1;
vegetable 0; meat 3; fat 1
Calories: 292

Chicken Veronique

2 whole chicken breasts, skinned
2 tablespoons margarine
1 cup fresh mushrooms, sliced
3 tablespoons green onion, sliced
¼ cup pimiento, minced
½ cup chicken broth
2 tablespoons all-purpose flour
1 cup seedless green grapes, halved
½ cup dry white wine
2 cups rice, cooked

Bone chicken breasts. Cut breasts into 1-in. pieces; set aside. In a skillet, melt margarine over medium-high heat. Saute mushrooms and onions in butter about 3 minutes or until soft. Add pimiento. Add chicken pieces and saute about 5 minutes or until chicken is done. Blend chicken broth and flour; add to chicken mixture. Cook and stir until thickened and bubbly; cook and stir 1 minute longer. Stir in grapes and wine; heat through. Serve at once over warm rice. Serves 4.

PER SERVING:
Cholesterol (mg): 34
Fat (grams): total 8; saturated 1
Exchanges: milk 0; fruit 0; bread/starch 2;
vegetable 0; meat 2; fat 0
Calories: 261

Cornish Hens with Orange Sauce

6 Cornish hens, cleaned and split
¼ lb. margarine, melted
1 cup fruit-only orange marmalade
¼ cup brown sugar
3 tablespoons wine vinegar
2 teaspoons Worcestershire sauce
½ teaspoon ginger, ground
3 tablespoons orange liqueur

Preheat oven to 350°. Wash and dry hens. Brush with melted margarine. Line broiler pan with aluminum foil. Place hen halves, skin side down, on pan. Combine marmalade, brown sugar, vinegar, Worcestershire sauce, ginger, and orange liqueur in saucepan. Heat over medium heat to boiling point. Simmer for 2 minutes, stirring constantly. Brush surface of hens with sauce. Bake 30 minutes. Turn; bake 30 minutes longer, brushing often with sauce. Serve with remaining sauce. Serves 6.

PER SERVING (3½ oz., without skin):
Cholesterol (mg): 52
Fat (grams): total 29; saturated 4
Exchanges: milk 0; fruit 0; bread/starch 3;
vegetable 0; meat 3; fat 4
Calories: 584

Turkey and Noodle Gratin
A great recipe for leftover turkey

6 ozs. no-yolk noodles
2 tablespoons olive oil
2 tablespoons margarine
2 tablespoons all-purpose flour
2 cups fresh turkey broth, or canned chicken
  broth

½ cup evaporated skim milk
¼ teaspoon red pepper flakes
½ teaspoon nutmeg
   White pepper, freshly ground to taste
3 tablespoons shallots, finely chopped
1 cup crushed canned tomatoes
3 cups turkey meat, cooked, skinned, boned,
   and cut into bite-size pieces
   Egg substitute equal to 1 egg, lightly beaten
2 tablespoons Parmesan cheese, freshly grated

Cook noodles according to package directions. Do not overcook. Drain and return to pot. Add 1 tablespoon olive oil and toss well.

Melt margarine in a saucepan and add flour, stirring with wire whisk. Blend well. Add broth, stirring rapidly with whisk. When sauce is thickened and smooth, simmer 5 minutes. Add evaporated skim milk, pepper flakes, nutmeg, and white pepper. Blend well with whisk and simmer briefly. Set cream sauce aside.

Heat remaining 1 tablespoon olive oil in a saucepan. Add shallots. Cook and stir briefly. Add tomatoes; stir and simmer for 10 minutes. Add turkey meat and 1 cup of cream sauce. Stir and blend gently. Add egg substitute to remaining cream sauce. Heat to a boil, stirring rapidly with whisk for 30 seconds. Pour turkey mixture into noodles, and cover with cream sauce. Top with grated Parmesan cheese. Serves 4–6.

PER SERVING:
Cholesterol (mg): 22
Fat (grams): total 13; saturated 2
Exchanges: milk 0; fruit 0; bread/starch 2;
vegetable 0; meat 1; fat 2
Calories: 305

The Best Roasted Chicken or Turkey

1 roasting chicken or small turkey (5–7 lbs.)
4 large garlic cloves, peeled
6 tablespoons Dijon mustard
1 teaspoon thyme
1 cup butter buds
　Oregano
　Garlic powder

Wash poultry and pat dry. Mince garlic and mix with mustard and thyme. Preheat oven to 400°.

Starting at chicken breast and working down to the leg area, separate skin from meat with your fingers; be careful not to tear skin. Spoon mustard mixture into space between skin and meat. Pour butter buds over chicken or turkey. Sprinkle with oregano and garlic powder.

Place breast side up in shallow roasting pan. Bake until juices run clear rather than pink when thigh is pierced with knife. Cook about 20 minutes per pound. Let rest 15 minutes before carving. Serves 4.

PER SERVING, Light Meat (3½-oz. portion):
Cholesterol (mg): 89
Fat (grams): total 7; saturated 2
Exchanges: milk 0; fruit 0; bread/starch 0;
vegetable 0; meat 3; fat 1
Calories: 190

PER SERVING, Dark Meat (3½-oz. portion):
Cholesterol (mg): 93
Fat (grams): total 10; saturated 3
Exchanges: milk 0; fruit 0; bread/starch 0;
vegetable 0; meat 3; fat 1
Calories: 205

Seafood

Americans are very fortunate to have a large and varied supply of fish and shellfish available for their dining pleasure. Seacoast towns have long been famous for their special seafood dishes, but now, due to innovations in packaging and transportation, every section of our wonderful country can enjoy delicious and healthful seafood at its freshest.

The following collection of recipes includes some old family favorites, such as bouillabaisse, adapted for a low-cholesterol diet, a delicious salmon flan, and an easy recipe for good old-fashioned tuna and noodles. You will also find recipes for sauces and fillings that will enhance the flavor of the fish and make your cooking become legendary. You can bake your fish or broil it, you can barbecue it or fill it with a special mixture, but all of these recipes, plain or fancy, will guarantee success.

Salmon Salad Platter

2 15½-oz. cans salmon

1 cup green onion, chopped

1 cup celery, chopped

¼ cup sweet pickle, chopped

1 tablespoon lemon juice

¼ cup whipped cottage cheese

¼ cup low-fat yogurt

1 can artichoke hearts

1 can asparagus

12 cherry tomatoes

2 cucumbers, sliced

6 radish roses

Drain salmon and flake. Place salmon, onion, celery, pickle, and lemon juice in a bowl. Set aside.

Place cottage cheese and yogurt in food processor or blender and blend until smooth. Add cottage cheese mixture to salmon and mix well.

Divide salmon mixture into 6 portions and place in mounds on 6 plates. Divide artichoke hearts, asparagus, tomatoes, cucumbers, and radishes among the plates in a decorative pattern and serve. Serves 6.

Note: This salmon salad is an excellent sandwich filling, delicious on whole-wheat or pita bread.

PER SERVING:
Cholesterol (mg): 53
Fat (grams): total 12; saturated 2
Exchanges: milk 0; fruit 0; bread/starch 0;
vegetable 1; meat 4; fat 1
Calories: 284

Salmon Flan
This is a great brunch dish

Vegetable cooking spray
2 tablespoons margarine
2 small onions, peeled and diced
6 egg whites
1 egg yolk
6¼ ozs. skinless, boneless pink salmon
½ cup evaporated skim milk
2 tablespoons low-fat yogurt
1 teaspoon dried dill
¼ teaspoon Spike

Preheat oven to 250°. Spray four 1-cup soufflé dishes or custard cups with vegetable cooking spray. Melt margarine in a small skillet and cook onion until soft, about 5 minutes. Whisk egg whites and yolk in a medium bowl. Add onion, salmon, skim milk, yogurt, and seasonings. Divide among soufflé dishes.

Recipe can be prepared a day ahead to this point. Cover tightly and refrigerate. Bake for 20 minutes. Stir gently, then continue baking until soufflés are set in the center, about 40 minutes longer, for a total of 60 minutes. Soufflés may be garnished with a dollop of yogurt and topped with a dill sprig. Serves 4.

PER SERVING:
Cholesterol (mg): 87
Fat (grams): total 13; saturated 3
Exchanges: milk 0; fruit 0; bread/starch 0;
vegetable 2; meat 3; fat 1
Calories: 261

Salmon Loaf with Two Sauces*

1 recipe White Sauce (pp. 210, 211)
1 recipe Dill Sauce (pg. 211)
1 16-oz. can salmon
2 egg whites, lightly beaten
2 tablespoons onion, minced
½ cup celery, chopped
2 tablespoons green bell pepper, minced
2 tablespoons chives, minced
1 teaspoon fresh dill
1 cup dried breadcrumbs
1 tablespoon fresh lemon juice
    Vegetable cooking spray

Heat oven to 350°. Drain salmon over bowl, reserving the juice. Add water to salmon juice to make ½ cup. Put salmon, ½ cup liquid, and remaining ingredients into bowl. Mix to blend. Turn into a mold, sprayed with vegetable cooking spray, or a 9x5-in. loaf pan. Bake until golden, 30–40 minutes.

Unmold and cool 5 minutes. To serve, cut into 1-in. slices. Pass both sauces so guests can select the one they want or some of both! Serves 6.

*Note: This loaf is good enough to serve without a sauce.

PER SERVING (without sauces):
Cholesterol (mg): 23
Fat (grams): total 9; saturated 2
Exchanges: milk 0; fruit 0; bread/starch 0;
vegetable 2; meat 2; fat 1
Calories: 198

Salmon Mousse

1 cup low-fat yogurt
1 10½-oz. can cream of mushroom soup
2 envelopes unflavored gelatin
¼ cup water
2 7¾-oz. cans boned, skinless salmon
½ cup celery, chopped
½ cup green onion, chopped
 1 cup whipped cottage cheese
½ teaspoon Spike
  Cucumber, green olives, pimiento (optional)

Spray a 5-quart fish mold with vegetable cooking spray and set aside.

Combine yogurt and soup in double boiler. Heat over medium heat until smooth.

Dissolve gelatin in water according to package directions, then add to soup mixture. Fold in remaining ingredients. Blend well and turn into a 5-quart mold. Refrigerate until firm. Garnish with thinly sliced cucumber, overlaping to form scales. You can use sliced green olives for eyes and pimiento strips for the tail. Serve with crackers, bagel chips, or party breads. Serves 4 (reduce portions if not served as main course).

PER SERVING (not including crackers or breads):
Cholesterol (mg): 4
Fat (grams): total 1; saturated 1
Exchanges: milk 0; fruit 0; bread/starch 0;
vegetable 0; meat 2; fat 0
Calories: 116

Special Salmon-Stuffed Potatoes

4 baking potatoes
1 can skinless, boneless pink salmon
Skim milk
2 tablespoons margarine
¼ cup onion, minced
1 cup Parmesan cheese, freshly grated
⅛ teaspoon pepper

Wash potatoes and bake at 450° for 50–60 minutes. Cut in half lengthwise; scoop out potato and mash, leaving shell intact. Reserve mashed potato. Drain salmon, reserving liquid; flake. Add milk to reserved liquid to equal ½ cup; combine with mashed potato, margarine, onion, ¼ cup of cheese, and pepper. Fold in salmon.

Spoon mixture into potato shells. Bake at 375° for 20 minutes or until filling is lightly browned. Sprinkle with remaining cheese; bake 5 minutes longer. Serves 4.

PER SERVING:
Cholesterol (mg): 54
Fat (grams): total 25; saturated 6
Exchanges: milk 0; fruit 0; bread/starch 1;
vegetable 0; meat 4; fat 3
Calories: 445

Spectacular Salmon Burgers

1 12½-oz. can boneless, skinless pink salmon;
  or 1½ cups cooked salmon
1 egg white, beaten
½ cup seasoned breadcrumbs
¼ cup onions, chopped
½ teaspoon dried thyme
½ teaspoon cracked pepper
1 teaspoon Spike
1 tablespoon corn oil
  Lettuce leaves
  Tomato slices
2 small pita bread rounds, halved crosswise
  Dill Sauce (pg. 211)

Drain the canned salmon, reserving 2 tablespoons of liquid. Or use two tablespoons of water if using fresh cooked salmon.

In a mixing bowl, stir together reserved liquid, egg white, breadcrumbs, onion, thyme, pepper, and Spike. Add drained salmon; mix well. Shape into four ½-in.-thick patties.

In a skillet, cook patties in hot oil over medium heat 2–3 minutes or until first side is brown. Turn and cook 2 minutes more until remaining side is brown. Serve each patty with lettuce and tomato in a pita half. Top with Dill Sauce. Serves 4.

PER SERVING:
Cholesterol (mg): 41
Fat (grams): total 10; saturated 2
Exchanges: milk 0; fruit 0; bread/starch 0;
vegetable 1; meat 3; fat 1
Calories: 237

Asparagus- and Mushroom-Stuffed Fish Rolls

4 fresh or frozen fish fillets, such as flounder,
   turbot, or monkfish
1 10-oz. pkg. frozen asparagus
4 green onions, halved lengthwise
½ cup mushrooms, chopped
2 teaspoons margarine
3 tablespoons dry white wine
¼ teaspoon Spike
¼ teaspoon garlic powder
2 tablespoons water
1 cup celery, chopped
1½ teaspoons cornstarch
1 tablespoon cold water
1 tomato, sliced
¼ cup parsley, chopped

Thaw fish if frozen. Cook asparagus and onions, covered, in a small amount of boiling water for about 3 minutes. Drain. Place in dish and add chopped mushrooms. Set aside.

Dot each fish fillet with ½ teaspoon of margarine. Place one-fourth of the asparagus-mushroom mixture across center of each fillet; roll up fish and fasten with wooden picks. Place rolls in a baking dish, about 8 in. square.

Combine wine, Spike, and garlic powder with the water and sprinkle over fish. Cover; bake in 400° oven 30–35 minutes. Remove fish to serving platter; keep warm.

Measure pan juices, adding enough water to equal ¾-cup liquid. Cook celery in the liquid for 5 minutes. Combine cornstarch and 1 tablespoon cold water; stir into the celery mixture. Cook and stir till bubbly. Cook 2 minutes more. Pour sauce over fish and garnish with tomato slices and parsley. Serves 4.

PER SERVING:
Cholesterol (mg): *60*

Fat (grams): total 10
Exchanges: milk 0; fruit 0; bread/starch 0;
vegetable 0; meat 4; fat 1
Calories: 250

Monkfish Florentine Saute

4 tablespoons margarine, melted
2 tablespoons olive oil
1 tablespoon shallots, minced
Flour and white pepper for dusting
1½ lbs. monkfish, cut into large chunks
1 large yellow bell pepper, cut into thin strips
1 large red bell pepper, cut into thin strips
½ lb. fresh spinach, washed and torn
½ cup mushrooms, sliced
2 fresh lemons, juiced

Put margarine and olive oil into a skillet and add shallots; cook until lightly browned. Turn heat up until a few drops of water thrown on surface will sizzle. Meanwhile, put flour and pepper into a plastic bag, add fish, and shake until lightly coated. Add monkfish and peppers to hot skillet and saute 4 minutes, shaking skillet vigorously. Add spinach, mushrooms, and lemon juice and stir until spinach wilts and sauce thickens. Serve immediately. Serves 4.

PER SERVING:
Cholesterol (mg): 60
Fat (grams): total 26; saturated 3
Exchanges: milk 0; fruit 0; bread/starch 0;
vegetable 0; meat 5; fat 3
Calories: 403

Baked Fish with Tomato Basil Sauce

TOMATO SAUCE

1 tablespoon olive oil
½ cup green onions, chopped
1 clove garlic, minced
2 9½-oz. cans whole tomatoes, drained and chopped
½ cup green bell pepper, minced
½ cup mushrooms, sliced
1 tablespoon basil
1 teaspoon cayenne pepper
1 teaspoon Spike
1 tablespoon fresh lemon juice

FISH

1½ lbs. whitefish fillets; or any similar fish, such as turbot, monkfish, or snapper
Juice of 1 lemon
½ cup dry white wine
4 tablespoons margarine, melted
2 tablespoons fresh parsley, chopped

Tomato Sauce: Heat oil in skillet over medium heat. Add onions and garlic; cook until onions are soft, about 5 minutes. Add tomatoes, green pepper, and mushrooms. Cook about 5 minutes. Add basil, pepper, and Spike. Cook, stirring, until mixture thickens slightly, about 8 minutes. Remove from heat. Stir in lemon juice.

Fish: Heat oven to 375°. Rinse fish with cold water. Pat dry on paper towel. Place fish in shallow baking dish. Sprinkle with lemon juice. Pour wine over fish and add melted margarine. Bake until fish flakes easily, about 10 minutes. Remove fish to warm serving platter and spoon tomato sauce on top of fish. Sprinkle with parsley. Serves 4.

PER SERVING:
Cholesterol (mg): 60
Fat (grams): total 23; saturated 2

Exchanges: *milk 0; fruit 0; bread/starch 0;*
vegetable 3; meat 4; fat 3
Calories: *419*

Tuna and Noodles

1 10½-oz. can chicken broth
1 12-oz. can evaporated skim milk
1 garlic clove, minced
¼ teaspoon white pepper
1 cup Parmesan cheese, freshly grated
8 ozs. no-yolk noodles
1 6½-oz. can tuna in spring water
¼ cup pimiento
½ cup Italian parsley, chopped

Bring chicken broth and evaporated skim milk to a
boil. Add garlic and white pepper. Cook and stir for 30 seconds. Remove from heat. Add Parmesan cheese; cover and
set aside for 5 minutes.

Cook noodles according to package directions. Drain
and keep warm.

Transfer sauce to blender; blend until smooth. Drain
and flake tuna. To assemble, place egg noodles on a warm
platter, top with sauce and tuna. Sprinkle with pimiento
and parsley. Serves 4.

PER SERVING:
Cholesterol (mg): *50*
Fat (grams): *total 9; saturated 5*
Exchanges: *milk 0; fruit 0; bread/starch 3;*
vegetable 1; meat 3; fat 1
Calories: *467*

✳

Tuna Almondine

2 **envelopes unflavored gelatin**
½ **cup cold water**
1 **cup boiling water**
1 **lb. low-fat cottage cheese, whipped**
2 **tablespoons lemon juice**
¼ **teaspoon garlic powder**
¼ **teaspoon Spike**
⅓ **cup green onions, finely chopped**
2 **tablespoons pimientos, chopped**
2 **7-oz. cans tuna, drained and flaked**
1 **cup almonds, sliced and lightly toasted**

Spray a 5½-cup fish mold with vegetable cooking spray and set aside.

In large bowl, sprinkle unflavored gelatin over cold water; let stand 1 minute. Add boiling water and stir until gelatin is completely dissolved. With rotary beater, blend in cottage cheese until smooth. Stir in lemon juice, garlic powder, and Spike. Fold in green onions, pimiento, tuna, and ½ cup of almonds.

Pour into a 5½-cup mold; chill until firm. Before serving, unmold onto a platter and garnish with remaining almonds, overlapping to form scales. Green olive slices can be used for the eyes, and additional pimiento can be used on the tail if desired. Serve with crackers, bagel chips, or party breads. Makes about 5½ cups, or 11 half-cup servings.

PER SERVING (one-half cup):
Cholesterol (mg): 22
Fat (grams): total 12; saturated 3
Exchanges: milk 0; fruit 0; bread/starch 0;
vegetable 1; meat 2; fat 1
Calories: 201

✳ Bouillabaisse

1 cup onions, chopped
½ cup celery, chopped
1 clove garlic, minced
¼ cup olive oil
2 packets Butter Buds
1 cup water
1 cup white wine
2 14½-oz. cans whole tomatoes
3 leeks (white portion), cleaned and finely
   sliced into matchsticks
1 bay leaf
1 teaspoon dried thyme
1 teaspoon orange peel, grated
3 lbs. fresh or frozen and thawed salmon,
   skinned, boned, and cubed
½ lb. imitation crab meat
½ lb. bay scallops
12 mussels
¼ cup parsley, chopped

In a Dutch oven over medium-high heat, saute onion, celery, and garlic in olive oil until tender, about 7 minutes. Add Butter Buds, water, and wine. Stir in tomatoes, leeks, herbs, and grated peel and bring to a boil. Reduce heat to low and simmer 10 minutes. Stir in salmon, crab, scallops, and mussels. Over high heat, return to a boil. Reduce heat to low and simmer 10 minutes more. Stir in parsley. Serves 8–10.

PER SERVING:
Cholesterol (mg): 71
Fat (grams): total 16; saturated 3
Exchanges: milk 0; fruit 0; bread/starch 0;
vegetable 2; meat 5; fat 1
Calories: 380

Pompano en Papillote

Parchment or foil wrap
1 stick margarine
¼ cup fresh parsley, chopped
¼ cup white wine
4 tablespoons garlic, minced
White pepper, dash
6 pompano fillets (or red snapper), about 7 ozs.
   each
4 medium tomatoes, sliced
2 large zucchini, julienned
2 leeks, julienned
Thyme leaves
Oregano leaves
2 tablespoons olive oil

Heat oven to 425°. Cut 6 pieces of parchment, each about 18x12 in. Fold each sheet in half and, using pinking shears, round off the unfolded edges. Unfold each sheet and set aside.

Place margarine in a mixing bowl. Add parsley, wine, and garlic and beat with a mixer for 15 minutes. Season with white pepper. Cover and store in refrigerator until ready to use.

Spread a teaspoon of the garlic margarine in center of one sheet. Place a fish fillet on the butter, and top with a tomato slice. Place 2 tablespoons of zucchini and leek on top of the tomato, and sprinkle with herbs. Drizzle olive oil over all. Repeat this procedure with remaining sheets.

Fold the paper over the fish and pinch edges at close intervals to seal them. Place packages on a cookie sheet. Cook fish for 10 minutes. Transfer packages to a dinner plate. Slice each open with a sharp knife, and fold back paper to let the aroma escape. Serves 6.

PER SERVING:
Cholesterol (mg): 50
Fat (grams): total 21; saturated 3

Exchanges: milk 0; fruit 0; bread/starch 0;
vegetable 1; meat 2; fat 3
Calories: 282

Crab Salad Louis

1 cup light mayonnaise
½ cup evaporated skim milk
¼ cup chili sauce
¼ cup green bell pepper, chopped
¼ cup green onions, chopped
2 tablespoons green olives, chopped
Juice of one-half lemon
Lettuce
2 cups imitation crab meat chunks
¼ cup chives, minced

For the dressing, mix all ingredients in a small bowl.
Line 4 individual bowls with lettuce. Toss crabmeat with
salad dressing. Spoon crabmeat salad into individual serving bowls and garnish with chives. Serves 4.

PER SERVING:
Cholesterol (mg): 14
Fat (grams): total 10; saturated 0
Exchanges: milk 0; fruit 0; bread/starch 1;
vegetable 1; meat 2; fat 0
Calories: 228

Baked Seafood Salad

1 small green bell pepper, chopped
1 small onion, chopped
1 cup celery, chopped
1 lb. imitation crab meat
1 lb. small scallops, cooked
1 cup Mock Sour Cream (pg. 214)
1 teaspoon Spike
1 teaspoon Worcestershire sauce
1 cup breadcrumbs
2 tablespoons margarine

Mix all ingredients in casserole. Sprinkle breadcrumbs on top. Dot with margarine. Bake for 30 minutes at 350°. Do not overbake. Serves 6.

PER SERVING:
Cholesterol (mg): 35
Fat (grams): total 6; saturated 0
Exchanges: milk 0; fruit 0; bread/starch 1;
vegetable 0; meat 3; fat 0
Calories: 255

Scallops à la Mushrooms

1 lb. bay scallops with natural broth
½ cup white wine
1 tablespoon fresh lemon juice
2 garlic cloves, minced
½ lb. mushrooms, sliced
4 scallions with tops, sliced
3 tablespoons chives, minced
2 tablespoons margarine
1 tablespoon flour

1 tablespoon parsley, minced
2 teaspoons Parmesan cheese, freshly grated
White pepper to taste
Seasoned breadcrumbs
Margarine

In large skillet, simmer scallops over low heat in their own broth, wine, and lemon juice. Cook 2–3 minutes, just until scallops become opaque. Do not overcook. Drain, reserving cooking liquid.

Saute garlic, mushrooms, scallions, and chives in margarine for 3–5 minutes. Remove vegetables from pan. Stir in flour. Stir in reserved cooking liquid, parsley, cheese, and pepper. Cook, stirring continuously, until sauce is smooth and thickened. Add scallops and mushroom mixture. Cook 1 minute until reheated.

Spoon mixture into individual baking shells. Sprinkle with seasoned breadcrumbs and dot with margarine. Brown slightly under broiler. Serve immediately. Serves 4.

PER SERVING:
Cholesterol (mg): 39
Fat (grams): total 6; saturated 1
Exchanges: milk 0; fruit 0; bread/starch 0;
vegetable 2; meat 3; fat 0
Calories: 200

Broiled Fish with White Sauce

1 recipe Basic White Sauce (pp. 210, 211)
6 6-oz. pieces of flounder, orange roughy, or
sole
Juice of 1 lemon
1 tablespoon corn oil
1 teaspoon lemon rind, grated
3 tablespoons dry white wine
¾ cup ripe tomato, finely chopped, peeled, and
seeded
2 tablespoons fresh dill, chopped
2 tablespoons Molly McButter*

Brush fish with lemon juice and with corn oil. Broil
until fish flakes easily, about 15 minutes. Heat sauce and
stir in remaining ingredients. Serve piping hot. Serves 6
Note: *Molly McButter is all natural butter-flavor sprinkles and is found in the seasoning and herb section of your
supermarket.

PER SERVING:
Cholesterol (mg): 50
Fat (grams): total 2; saturated 0
Exchanges: milk 0; fruit 0; bread/starch 0;
vegetable 0; meat 4; fat 0
Calories: 220

Pasta and Rice

I can honestly say that I am passionate about pasta. I can see why it has become the "in food." Pasta is a simple, basic food but so versatile that it is a cook's dream. Pasta can be layered, rolled, stuffed, boiled, and baked. It can be served hot or cold. Pasta is economical and quick and easy to cook. Men and children love it.

The best news is that pasta does not contain any cholesterol in itself. If you select the right topping, you will have a dish that is both cholesterol free and delicious.

Pasta allows any cook the pleasure of being creative. You can entertain with pasta from the very simple tomato-basil sauce to the very elaborate and expensive sauces made from caviar, truffles, lobster, shrimp, or salmon. While pasta is inexpensive, let me caution you not to select pasta solely on the basis of price. It is my belief that the best pasta is made from 100 percent *durum semolina* wheat. It is also important to know that white flour pasta is not only mushy but also very high in calories and does not have the full complement of nutrients you expect in pasta.

One of the most important requirements in cooking pasta is to select the right size pot. A four-quart pot is sufficient to cook one pound of pasta properly. Use a larger pot when cooking more than one pound. Fill the pot to within three inches of the top with cold water. Cover the pot and bring the water to a boil. (There is no need to add oil to the water; the addition of salt is optional.) When the water boils, add the pasta, and, using a wooden fork, stir it immediately to prevent sticking.

Pasta should always be cooked and served *al dente*. Al dente refers to cooked pasta that is firm and chewy. Cooking pasta is easy if you are careful and watch the time. Test the pasta by biting into a piece to see whether it has the firmness you want.

Rice, like pasta, is a very versatile food. Rice can be simple as in Dirty Rice or elegant as in Risotto à la Maria. Your imagination should be your guide. Just as with pasta, you can make a rice dish that is inexpensive such as one made with butter, cheese, or herbs or an expensive dish made with caviar, porcini mushrooms, seafood, or goat cheese.

Rice comes in several varieties and you will need to consider the dish you are making before selecting the rice. For example, when making an Italian Risotto you are advised to buy Arborio rice because it holds al dente texture during the long cooking process. This type of rice is very nutritious and low in calories. You will also need long-grain, brown, and wild rice to round out your menus.

My wish is that you will take the time to develop your own pasta and rice dishes to create wonderful meals that are virtually cholesterol free. You will find that you can even throw a party utilizing pasta as the theme, with a number of different sauces, to economically feed a great many people in a magnificent way.

Spaghetti and Meatballs

SAUCE

1 double recipe Ultra Chic Marinara Sauce (pg. 213)

MEATBALLS

1 lb. ground turkey
½ lb. ground round
1 small onion, minced
1 clove garlic, minced
½ teaspoon oregano
½ teaspoon basil
½ teaspoon pepper
¼ cup breadcrumbs
3 tablespoons olive oil

SPAGHETTI

1 lb. thin spaghetti
Parsley, chopped

Sauce: Prepare sauce and set aside.

Meatballs: Mix all meatball ingredients in a medium bowl. Form into 1½-in. round meatballs. Arrange in a single layer in non-stick skillet. Fry in olive oil over medium heat, turning often until golden on all sides, about 15 minutes. Transfer to paper towel.

Add meatballs to Marinara Sauce and simmer 30 minutes more.

Spaghetti: Cook spaghetti in boiling water until *al dente.* Drain; toss with about ½ cup of sauce for each serving. Serve with meatballs. Sprinkle parsley on top. Serves 6-8.

PER SERVING:

Cholesterol (mg): 72

Fat (grams): total 12; saturated 4

Exchanges: milk 0; fruit 0; bread/starch 3;
vegetable 1; meat 2; fat 1

Calories: 430

Spaghettini Arrabbiata

SPAGHETTINI

1 lb. thin spaghetti
4 tablespoons extra virgin olive oil
4 cloves garlic, minced
1 red bell pepper, cut in thin strips
1 yellow bell pepper, cut in thin strips
1 green bell pepper, cut in thin strips
½ yellow squash, sliced thin
2 cups broccoli, florets only
1 cup mushrooms, sliced
½ cup Parmesan cheese, freshly grated
  Fresh basil leaves

DRESSING

½ cup olive oil
¼ cup raspberry or tarragon vinegar
2 cloves garlic, minced
1 tablespoon lemon juice
  Worcestershire sauce, dash
1 teaspoon parsley, chopped
1 teaspoon basil
¼ teaspoon tarragon
¼ teaspoon thyme
½ teaspoon white pepper
1 teaspoon Dijon mustard

Spaghettini: Put a large pot of water on the stove to boil for the spaghetti while you prepare the vegetables.

Saute garlic in olive oil for a minute or two. Add peppers and squash and simmer for 5 minutes. Add broccoli and mushrooms and saute for about 10 minutes. Remove from heat and keep warm while pasta cooks. Place pasta in large bowl and top with vegetables. Spoon on dressing and toss well. Sprinkle on Parmesan cheese, garnish with basil leaves, and serve immediately. Serves 6.

Dressing: Blend all ingredients in a blender until smooth.

PER SERVING:
Cholesterol (mg): 0
Fat (grams): total 28; saturated 4
Exchanges: milk 0; fruit 0; bread/starch 3;
vegetable 1; meat 0; fat 5
Calories: 493

Pasta with Garlic Sauce

2 cups low-fat cottage cheese
4 tablespoons evaporated skim milk
 White pepper, dash
8 cloves garlic, minced
2 teaspoons Tamari soy sauce
3 tablespoons chives, minced
1 lb. pkg. thin spaghetti
3 tablespoons Italian parsley, chopped
½ cup Parmesan cheese grated

Place first 6 ingredients in blender or food processor. Mix until completely smooth.

Place in a double boiler on medium heat. Heat until bubbly around edges. Cook spaghetti, pour on sauce, and toss gently. Garnish with parsley. Sprinkle with Parmesan cheese. Serve immediately. Serves 4.

PER SERVING:
Cholesterol (mg): 25
Fat (grams): total 9; saturated 5
Exchanges: milk 0; fruit 0; bread/starch 2;
vegetable 0; meat 3; fat 0
Calories: 307

Spaghetti with Uncooked Tomato Sauce

Make this when fresh tomatoes are at their peak

1 lb. thin spaghetti

1 lb. very ripe tomatoes, peeled, seeded, and
   diced*

3 cloves garlic, crushed

3 tablespoons olive oil

5 fresh basil leaves, chopped

½ cup black olives, sliced

1 cup Parmesan cheese, freshly grated

Pepper to taste

Boil water to cook the pasta.

Drop tomatoes into a small pan of boiling water; remove the skins, seed, and chop. Place in a bowl with the crushed garlic, olive oil, and chopped basil leaves. Stir often to blend the tastes. Add olives and toss well. This sauce can be placed in the refrigerator for several hours to marinate, which will enhance flavor.

Cook and drain pasta, and put it in a large pasta bowl. Pour the tomato sauce over the pasta, and toss with Parmesan cheese and pepper. Serve warm or at room temperature. Serves 6.

*Note: Fresh tomatoes are a must.

PER SERVING:

Cholesterol (mg): 9

Fat (grams): total 15; saturated 3

Exchanges: milk 0; fruit 0; bread/starch 3;
vegetable 1; meat 0; fat 3

Calories: 394

Featherweight Lasagna

6 cups Ultra Chic Marinara Sauce (pg. 213)
½ lb. dry lasagna noodles
1 lb. part-skim mozzarella cheese, divided into thirds
½ lb. part-skim ricotta cheese, divided into thirds
2 ozs. Parmesan cheese, freshly grated, divided

Cook lasagna noodles according to package directions. Drain.

Cover bottom of a 13x9-in. baking dish with one-fourth of the Marinara Sauce. Add a layer of lasagna noodles, trimming edges to fit the dish. Top with a layer of mozzarella cheese, then a layer of ricotta cheese. Sprinkle with Parmesan cheese. Repeat this procedure until all lasagna and cheese are used.

Bake at 350° for 45 minutes. Let stand 10 minutes before serving. Serves 12.

PER SERVING:
Cholesterol (mg): 32
Fat (grams): total 18; saturated 8
Exchanges: milk 0; fruit 0; bread/starch 1; vegetable 2; meat 2; fat 2
Calories: 348

Vegetable Lasagna

1 lb. lasagna noodles (or spinach lasagna noodles)
1 cup green onions, diced
3 cloves garlic, crushed
2 cups fresh mushrooms, sliced
2 tablespoons olive oil
2 lbs. fresh spinach leaves, without stems
1 teaspoon oregano
¼ teaspoon cayenne pepper
1 cup low-fat cottage cheese
½ cup Parmesan cheese, freshly grated
1 cup pimientos, minced
1 cup fresh Italian parsley, chopped
½ cup part-skim mozzarella cheese, shredded

Preheat oven to 350°. Boil water to cook the pasta in a large pot.

In a large skillet, saute the green onions, garlic, and mushrooms in the oil for 3 minutes. Add spinach leaves, oregano, and cayenne pepper and continue cooking, covered, for 5 minutes. Remove from heat.

Put cottage cheese, Parmesan cheese, and pimientos in a large bowl and blend thoroughly with parsley until well mixed. Drain lasagna noodles and rinse in cold water. Line noodles on a flat surface.

Layer noodles in a 2-quart baking dish. Spoon a layer of spinach mixture over noodles, then a layer of about ¼ cup of cottage cheese mixture and 2 tablespoons Parmesan cheese. Make three layers of lasagna noodles, spinach mixture, and cottage cheese mixture with Parmesan cheese. After layering the lasagna noodles and mixtures, top with shredded mozzarella and pimiento bits. Bake 8 to 10 minutes.

Let lasagna set and cool for 10 minutes before cutting and serving. Serves 8.

PER SERVING:
Cholesterol (mg): 13
Fat (grams): total 9; saturated 3

*Exchanges: milk 0; fruit 0; bread/starch 3;
vegetable 0; meat 2; fat 0*
Calories: 337

Pasta Primavera

1 lb. fettucini
¼ cup olive oil
2 cloves garlic, chopped
½ teaspoon oregano
½ teaspoon basil
1 cup broccoli florets
1 cup cauliflower florets
1 cup artichoke hearts
1 cup asparagus spears, cut in 1-in. pieces
1 cup green bell peppers, chopped
1 cup cherry tomatoes, halved
½ cup Parmesan cheese, freshly grated

Cook fettucini in boiling salted water until *al dente.*
As pasta cooks, heat olive oil in large skillet and saute garlic for 2 to 3 minutes. Add herbs and vegetables and saute
quickly over high heat until vegetables are tender but crisp.
Toss drained pasta with vegetables. Sprinkle with Parmesan cheese. Serves 6.

PER SERVING:
Cholesterol (mg): 2
Fat (grams): total 12; saturated 0
*Exchanges: milk 0; fruit 0; bread/starch 3;
vegetable 2; meat 0; fat 2*
Calories: 366

Fettucini with Scallops

1 cup water
1 cup dry white wine
1 tablespoon lemon juice
1½ lbs. bay scallops
1 medium onion, minced
2 large cloves garlic, minced
3 tablespoons olive oil
2 cups pea pods
1 cup radishes, sliced
3 cups asparagus, cut in 1-in. pieces
2 cups mushrooms, sliced
1 cup artichoke hearts
½ cup chicken stock
2 tablespoons fresh basil, chopped
1 cup evaporated skim milk
1 lb. fettucini, cooked and drained
1 cup Parmesan cheese, freshly grated

In a large saucepan, combine water, wine, and lemon juice. Bring to boil. Remove from heat, add scallops, and let steep 30 minutes. Drain.

In a large skillet or wok, saute onion and garlic in olive oil until onion is soft, about 2 minutes. Add pea pods, radishes, asparagus, and mushrooms. Stir-fry 2 minutes. Add artichoke hearts. Stir-fry 2 minutes more. Stir in chicken stock and basil. Simmer 3 minutes. Add scallops and milk. Simmer 1 minute.

Combine pasta with scallop mixture, tossing until well mixed. Pour into large serving bowl. Add cheese and toss again. Serve immediately. Serves 6.

PER SERVING:
Cholesterol (mg): 39
Fat (grams): total 10; saturated 2
Exchanges: milk 0; fruit 0; bread/starch 4;
vegetable 2; meat 3; fat 0
Calories: 510

Macaroni and Four Cheeses

1 cup macaroni
1 tablespoon margarine
½ cup Parmesan cheese, freshly grated
½ cup Romano cheese, freshly grated
1½ cups skim milk
1 cup low-fat cottage cheese
2 tablespoons all-purpose flour
4 thin onion slices
½ teaspoon dry mustard
½ cup part-skim mozzarella cheese, shredded
½ cup cracker crumbs or breadcrumbs
1 tablespoon margarine, melted

Cook macaroni; drain. Toss with 1 tablespoon margarine. In a 2-qt. baking dish, layer half the macaroni, Parmesan, and Romano cheeses. Add remaining macaroni and Parmesan and Romano cheeses.

In a blender container, blend the milk, cottage cheese, flour, onion, and mustard. Blend until smooth. Pour over layered macaroni. Sprinkle mozzarella cheese over top. Combine crumbs and melted margarine; sprinkle on top.

Bake at 350° for 40 minutes. Serves 6.

PER SERVING:
Cholesterol (mg): 36
Fat (grams): total 15; saturated 8
Exchanges: milk 0; fruit 0; bread/starch 2;
vegetable 1; meat 2; fat 2
Calories: 400

Italian Macaroni and Beans

2 cloves garlic, minced
2 tablespoons olive oil
2 cups Ultra Chic Marinara Sauce (pg. 213)
1 teaspoon oregano
1 teaspoon garlic powder
1 16-oz. can cannellini beans
½ lb. elbow macaroni, uncooked
    Salt, pepper to taste
    Parsley, freshly chopped
    Parmesan cheese, freshly grated
    Italian bread, optional

In a saucepan, saute garlic gently in oil until golden brown. Add Marinara Sauce and cook 10 minutes. Stir in spices. Add beans; stir gently and continue to simmer.

Cook macaroni in boiling water until *al dente.* Drain, salt and pepper to taste, and add to bean mixture. Stir gently. If mixture gets too thick, add a little water. Add parsley and stir well.

Place macaroni and beans in a large bowl and sprinkle with Parmesan cheese. Serve immediately or the pasta will absorb all the liquid. Use Italian bread for dunking. Serves 6.

PER SERVING:
Cholesterol (mg): 2
Fat (grams): total 11; saturated 2
Exchanges: milk 0; fruit 0; bread/starch 3;
vegetable 0; meat 0; fat 2
Calories: 336

Roman Macaroni Casserole

CASSEROLE
- 1 lb. ziti (macaroni), broken up
- 2 tablespoons margarine, melted
- 1 cup Parmesan cheese, freshly grated
- 1 lb. part-skim mozzarella cheese, shredded

SAUCE
- 4 tablespoons margarine
- 1 onion, chopped
- 1 garlic clove, whole
- ½ cup Bertani Soave (or other dry white wine)
- 1½ cups canned tomatoes, chopped
- ½ teaspoon basil
- Cayenne pepper, dash

Casserole: Cook the ziti *al dente* in salted water, drain, and return to pot. Add melted margarine and mix well with two wooden spoons to coat ziti thoroughly. Butter a heat-resistant casserole and put in a layer of ziti; sprinkle on a little Parmesan cheese and mozzarella. Spread a few tablespoons of the Sauce over top. Repeat procedure in layers until you have used up all ziti, cheeses, and sauce. End with a top layer of mozzarella, Parmesan, and sauce. Put casserole into preheated 400° oven and bake 10 minutes. Serve from casserole. Serves 6.

Sauce: In the margarine, saute onion and garlic until browned. Discard garlic. Add wine and stir. Cook over low heat for 3 minutes. Add tomatoes, basil, and pepper; stir well and cook slowly for 35 minutes.

PER SERVING:
Cholesterol (mg): 48
Fat (grams): total 28; saturated 12
Exchanges: milk 0; fruit 0; bread/starch 3;
vegetable 1; meat 2; fat 5
Calories: 612

Rigatoni with Vegetables

2 tablespoons margarine
2 tablespoons olive oil
1 tablespoon parsley, chopped
1 clove garlic, minced
½ cup onions, chopped
3 carrots, minced
¼ head cabbage, shredded
1 zucchini, cubed
3 large tomatoes, peeled and cubed
½ cup chicken stock
1 tablespoon basil
½ tablespoon chervil
   Pepper to taste
1 tablespoon Spike
1 tablespoon oregano
1 lb. rigatoni, uncooked
¾ cup Romano cheese, freshly grated
¾ cup Parmesan cheese, freshly grated
¼ cup margarine, softened

Place the 2 tablespoons of margarine and oil in a large saucepan, heat, and add parsley, garlic, onions, and carrots and cook until soft. Add cabbage, zucchini, tomatoes, stock, and seasonings. Cover and cook slowly for 45 minutes, stirring occasionally.

Cook rigatoni *al dente*, drain, and place in a bowl. Pour cheeses and softened margarine over pasta. Mix well, stir in vegetable sauce, and toss. Serve in large individual bowls that have been warmed. Serves 8.

PER SERVING:
Cholesterol (mg): 27
Fat (grams): total 20; saturated 8
Exchanges: milk 0; fruit 0; bread/starch 2;
vegetable 1; meat 1; fat 3
Calories: 398

Vegetable-Stuffed Shells

24 jumbo pasta shells, uncooked
1 10-oz. pkg. frozen chopped spinach, thawed
1 egg white
1½ cups low-fat cottage cheese
1½ cups part-skim mozzarella cheese, shredded
⅓ cup onion, finely chopped
2 cloves garlic, minced
⅓ cup parsley, chopped
1 10-oz. pkg. chopped broccoli, thawed
2 cups Ultra Chic Marinara Sauce (pg. 213)
½ cup Parmesan cheese, freshly grated

Prepare pasta shells according to package directions. Squeeze spinach to remove as much moisture as possible. Combine spinach, egg white, cottage and mozzarella cheeses, onion, garlic, parsley, and broccoli. Blend well.

Stuff shells with cottage cheese mixture, using about 2 tablespoons for each shell. Arrange in a 13x9-in. pan sprayed with vegetable cooking spray. Pour Marinara Sauce over shells. Sprinkle with Parmesan cheese. Bake, covered, at 350° for 30–40 minutes. Serves 8.

PER SERVING:
Cholesterol (mg): 23
Fat (grams): total 12; saturated 5
Exchanges: milk 0; fruit 0; bread/starch 2;
vegetable 0; meat 3; fat 1
Calories: 397

✳
Dirty Rice

2 teaspoons red pepper (preferably cayenne), ground

1½ teaspoons black pepper

1¼ teaspoons sweet paprika

1 teaspoon dry mustard

1 teaspoon cumin, ground

½ teaspoon dried thyme leaves

½ teaspoon oregano leaves

2 tablespoons vegetable oil

¼ lb. chicken, ground

2 bay leaves

½ cup onions, finely chopped

½ cup celery, finely chopped

½ cup green bell pepper, finely chopped

2 teaspoons garlic, minced

2 tablespoons margarine

2 cups chicken stock

¾ cup rice (preferably converted), uncooked

Combine first 7 seasoning ingredients in a small bowl and set aside. Place ground chicken and bay leaves in large skillet with oil; cook over high heat until meat is thoroughly browned, about 8 minutes, stirring occasionally.

Stir in the seasoning mix, then add onions, celery, peppers, and garlic; stir thoroughly, scraping pan bottom well. Add margarine and stir until melted. Reduce heat to medium and cook about 10 minutes, stirring constantly and scraping pan bottom well.

Add chicken stock and stir until any mixture sticking to pan bottom comes loose. Cook about 8 minutes over high heat, stirring once. Add rice and stir thoroughly; cover pan and turn heat to very low; cook 5 minutes. Remove from heat and leave covered until rice is tender, about 10 minutes. Remove bay leaves and serve immediately. Serves 8.

PER SERVING:
Cholesterol (mg): 11
Fat (grams): total 8; saturated 1
Exchanges: milk 0; fruit 0; bread/starch 0;
vegetable 1; meat 1; fat 1
Calories: 121

Arroz con Tomate *(Spanish Rice)*

½ cup green pepper, chopped
¼ cup onion, chopped
 1 clove garlic, minced
½ teaspoon dried basil, crushed
½ teaspoon dried rosemary, crushed
 2 tablespoons olive oil
 2 cups water
 1 cup long-grain rice, uncooked
 1 cup tomato, chopped and peeled
   Pepper, dash
   Tomato slices

In a skillet, cook chopped green pepper, chopped onion, garlic, basil, and rosemary in hot olive oil until vegetables are tender. Stir in water, uncooked rice, chopped tomato, and pepper. Cover and cook over low heat about 20 minutes or until rice is done. Garnish with tomato slices and serve. Serves 6.

PER SERVING:
Cholesterol (mg): 0
Fat (grams): total 5; saturated less than 1
Exchanges: milk 0; fruit 0; bread/starch 0;
vegetable 2; meat 0; fat 1
Calories: 83

✳
Risotto à la Maria

¾ cup evaporated skim milk
3¼ cups chicken broth, divided
  4 tablespoons margarine, divided
   White pepper, dash
  2 large stalks broccoli (buds cut off and re-
    served), peeled and diced
  2 cups asparagus buds
  1 small red bell pepper, seeded and diced
1½ cups green onion, chopped (white and
    green parts)
  ¼ teaspoon red pepper flakes
  1 large clove garlic, minced
  2 tablespoons olive oil
  1 cup rice (Arborio preferred)
  ¼ cup vermouth
  1 cup peas (cooked if fresh; at room tempera-
    ture if frozen)
  ½ cup Parmesan cheese, freshly grated
  ¼ cup parsley, chopped

In a saucepan, combine milk, ¼ cup chicken broth, 2 tablespoons margarine, and 3 or 4 grinds of white pepper. Bring liquid to a simmer and cook until reduced by half. Set aside.

In another pan, bring water to a boil. Insert a steamer basket and cook the vegetables, separately, until crisp-tender. Begin with the diced broccoli and asparagus buds, then steam the diced red bell pepper and chopped onion.

In a saute pan, heat red pepper flakes and garlic in olive oil until garlic is soft. Turn off heat and add cooked vegetables to the pan. (Recipe may be done ahead to this point).

Heat remaining 2 tablespoons margarine in a heavy-bottomed saucepan. Add rice and stir to coat the grains with margarine. Add vermouth and stir over low heat until it evaporates. Now add ⅓ cup of remaining chicken broth. Stir until it is nearly absorbed, then add more broth. Repeat process, stirring frequently, until all broth has been added and rice is *al dente* (grains retain some firmness in their center). If necessary, continue process with more broth or water. It should take about 20 minutes.

During final 5 minutes of preparing the risotto, reheat milk mixture and vegetables over low heat. Add peas to milk to heat through. Stir milk and vegetable mixtures into risotto. Add cheese and parsley and stir well. Serve immediately. Serves 4.

PER SERVING:
Cholesterol (mg): 6
Fat (grams): total 22; saturated 3
Exchanges: milk 0; fruit 0; bread/starch 1; vegetable 0; meat 1; fat 4
Calories: 310

Vegetarian Dishes

One of the things I like best about vegetarian meals is that I don't have to remember to take meat out of the freezer to defrost. A more important benefit is that a vegetarian meal is usually lower in cholesterol, fat, and calories than dishes made with meat. In fact, vegetables are great for anyone monitoring cholesterol because they are choles-terol-free. Adding vegetarian dishes to your weekly menu can also result in effortless weight loss. Vegetarian meals are economical, too, much less expensive than steak or roast beef, yet so delicious.

You will want to experiment with these recipes and develop a few of your own. Some of these recipes can be used for appetizers as well as main dishes. You will find more vegetarian dishes in the "Pasta and Rice" chapter of this cookbook.

I think you should plan to start your new heart-health eating plan by trying to incorporate at least two vegetarian meals a week into your lifestyle. You will find this easy to do because many of these dishes do not require too many ingredients and are quick to prepare. They also freeze well, so you can prepare enough for more than one meal. I always like to cook enough for two meals.

Try to invite a few friends and plan a party around vegetarian dishes. These recipes are so delicious no one will complain that you did not serve meat.

Vegetable Paella
This is a one dish meal. Add a salad and crusty bread and enjoy

¾ lb. broccoli, sliced; or 1 10-oz. pkg. frozen
    chopped broccoli
2 small zucchini, sliced thin
1 medium green bell pepper, chopped
1 medium red bell pepper, chopped
½ cup onion, chopped
2 cloves garlic, minced
¼ cup olive oil
1 16-oz. can chopped tomatoes
    Black pepper to taste
2¾ cups chicken broth
1½ cups Arborio rice*
1 tablespoon lemon juice
1 cup frozen peas, thawed
⅔ cup Parmesan cheese, freshly grated

*Note: Arborio is an Italian rice found in specialty stores. It is best for this recipe because it can absorb a lot of liquid without becoming mushy.

Cook fresh broccoli in a small amount of boiling water for 5 minutes or until tender-crisp. If using frozen broccoli, cook according to package directions. Drain and reserve.

In a paella pan or a 12-in. oven-proof skillet, cook zucchini, green and red peppers, onion, and garlic in olive oil until onion is tender. Stir in undrained tomatoes and pepper. Stir in chicken broth, uncooked rice, and lemon juice; mix well. Bring to boiling. Reduce heat and simmer until rice is tender, about 20 minutes.

Bake, covered, in a 350° oven for 10 minutes. Stir in broccoli, peas, and Parmesan cheese. Serves 6.

PER SERVING:
Cholesterol (mg): 9
Fat (grams): total 13; saturated 4
Exchanges: milk 0; fruit 0; bread/starch 1;
vegetable 1; meat 1; fat 2
Calories: 230

Crepes Florentine with Spinach Filling

CREPES
1⅓ cups all-purpose flour
¼ teaspoon salt
1½ cups skim milk
2 teaspoons vegetable oil
3 egg whites, beaten
1 egg yolk, beaten
Vegetable cooking spray

SPINACH FILLING
3 tablespoons margarine
3 tablespoons all-purpose flour
1 cup skim milk
¾ cup water

¼ teaspoon nutmeg
3 tablespoons Parmesan cheese
1 10-oz. pkg. frozen chopped spinach, cooked

Crepes: Combine flour and salt in a small bowl; stir well. Gradually add milk, oil, and eggs. Beat, using a wire whisk, until smooth. Cover and chill at least 1 hour and up to 24 hours.

Coat a 10-in. crepe pan or non-stick skillet with cooking spray and place over medium-high heat until hot. Remove pan from heat and spoon 3 tablespoons batter into pan; quickly tilt pan in all directions so batter covers bottom with a thin film. Cook about 1 minute. Lift edge of crepe to test for doneness. Crepe is ready for turning when it can be shaken loose from pan. Turn crepe and cook 30 seconds on other side.

Place crepes on a towel and allow to cool. Repeat procedure until all batter is used. Stack crepes between layers of wax paper to prevent sticking. Makes about 15, 8-in. crepes.

Crepes can be frozen easily. Stack between single layers of wax paper, and wrap in plastic wrap. Seal in an airtight container to freeze up to 1 month. Thaw frozen crepes 1 hour at room temperature before using.

Spinach Filling: Melt margarine and add flour, stirring constantly until flour is well mixed and slightly cooked, about 2 minutes. Add milk slowly, continuing to mix. When it starts to thicken slightly, add water, nutmeg, and cheese. Cook until sauce thickens again slightly, about 5 minutes. Add sauce to the cooked and drained spinach. Makes filling for 6 large crepes.

To assemble crepes: Spoon ⅓ cup spinach filling down center of crepe, roll up, and place, seam side down, on serving plates. Top with a dollop of filling.

PER SERVING (one filled crepe):
Cholesterol (mg): *47*
Fat (grams): *total 9; saturated 2*
Exchanges: *milk 0; fruit 0; bread/starch 2;*
vegetable 0; meat 1; fat 1
Calories: *250*

✳
Stuffed Cabbage Leaves

1¼ cups raw brown rice
¼ cup mushrooms, chopped
1 onion, chopped
½ cup raisins
¼ cup dried currants
1 tablespoon caraway seeds
1 15-oz. can tomato sauce
12 whole cabbage leaves, steamed briefly
1 cup low-fat yogurt (optional)

Cook rice until done. Saute mushrooms and onion. Mix rice with mushrooms, onion, raisins, currants, and caraway seed. Add enough tomato sauce to moisten mixture.

Steam cabbage for a few minutes until leaves can be separated. Place about 3 tablespoons rice mixture on each leaf. Roll up and secure with a toothpick, if necessary.

Place rolled leaves in a covered skillet and pour remaining tomato sauce over all. Cook about 15 minutes or until cabbage is tender. This is especially good topped with yogurt. Serves 6.

PER SERVING:
Cholesterol (mg): 0
Fat (grams): total 1; saturated less than 1
Exchanges: milk 0; fruit 0; bread/starch 3;
vegetable 0; meat 0; fat 0
Calories: 232

✳

Eggplant Parmigiana

Vegetable cooking spray
1 teaspoon olive oil
1½ cups onions, minced
2 cloves garlic, minced
3 medium tomatoes (about 1½ lbs.), unpeeled, quartered
½ teaspoon dried whole oregano
1 bay leaf
1 teaspoon garlic powder
1 teaspoon basil
1 lb. eggplant, unpeeled, cut into 12, ½-in. slices
1 egg white, lightly beaten
½ cup fine, dry breadcrumbs
1 cup part-skim mozzarella cheese
½ cup Parmesan cheese, freshly grated

Coat a large non-stick skillet with cooking spray; add oil and place over medium-high heat until hot. Add onions and garlic; saute 5 minutes or until tender. Add tomatoes and next 4 ingredients; cover and cook about 25 minutes or until tomatoes are tender. Remove from heat; discard bay leaf.

Position rotary knife blade in food processor; add tomato mixture. Cover and process until smooth. Pour into a 12x8x2-in. baking dish, and set aside.

Dip eggplant slices in egg white; dredge in breadcrumbs. Place on rack of a broiler pan coated with cooking spray; broil 4 in. from heat about 3 minutes on each side. Arrange eggplant slices on tomato mixture; bake at 450° for 10 minutes. Sprinkle with both cheeses and bake an additional 5 minutes or until lightly browned. Serves 6.

PER SERVING:
Cholesterol (mg): 14
Fat (grams): total 6; saturated 3
Exchanges: milk 0; fruit 0; bread/starch 0;
vegetable 3; meat 1; fat 1
Calories: 158

✳
Vegetable Burgers

2 cups carrots, shredded
1 cup brown rice, cooked and cooled
½ cup onion, chopped
½ cup zucchini, chopped
½ cup fine dry breadcrumbs
1 tablespoon parsley, snipped
½ teaspoon garlic powder
1 teaspoon Spike
2 egg whites, beaten
2 tablespoons Tamari soy sauce
1 tablespoon Worcestershire sauce
   Non-stick vegetable cooking spray
6 tomato slices, for garnish

In a large bowl, stir together carrots, rice, onion, zucchini, breadcrumbs, parsley, garlic powder, and Spike. Stir together egg whites, soy sauce, and Worcestershire sauce; add to rice mixture. Mix well. Cover and chill. Shape into 6 patties.

Spray a baking sheet with non-stick vegetable cooking spray. Place patties on baking sheet. Broil 3–4 in. from heat for 3–5 minutes on each side or until set. To serve, top each patty with a tomato slice. Serves 6.

PER SERVING:
Cholesterol (mg): 0
Fat (grams): total 1; saturated 0
Exchanges: milk 0; fruit 0; bread/starch 1;
vegetable 0; meat 0; fat 0
Calories: 101

Asparagus Pie

¼ lb. fresh asparagus
1 cup low-fat cottage cheese
1 tablespoon lemon juice
3 tablespoons onions, minced
1 tablespoon fresh dillweed, minced
    Egg substitute equal to 1 egg, slightly beaten
2 sheets frozen phyllo pastry, thawed
    Vegetable cooking spray, butter-flavored
½ cup fresh parsley, snipped

Snap off tough ends of asparagus. Cook asparagus, covered, in small amount of boiling water 8 minutes or until crisp-tender. Drain well; set aside.

Combine next 5 ingredients in a small bowl; stir until well blended and set aside.

You will need to work with 1 phyllo sheet at a time. Begin by lightly spraying each sheet with cooking spray; fold in half crosswise, and lightly spray again with cooking spray. Set aside. Repeat procedure with remaining phyllo.

Place phyllo sheets, one on top of the other, on a baking sheet coated with cooking spray. Spoon cottage cheese mixture over half of phyllo to within ½ in. of edges; top with asparagus. Using a spatula, lift unfilled half of phyllo and fold over asparagus, tucking edges under to seal.

Lightly spray phyllo with cooking spray; bake at 350° for 40 minutes or until golden. Remove from oven; let stand 5 minutes. Garnish with parsley. Serve warm, using a sharp knife. Serves 2.

PER SERVING:
Cholesterol (mg): 5
Fat (grams): total 18
Exchanges: milk 0; fruit 0; bread/starch 2;
vegetable 0; meat 2; fat 2
Calories: 366

Hearty Bean Stew
Serve a hearty homemade bread and fresh fruit with this meatless stew

½ cup dry garbanzo beans
½ cup dry kidney beans
3 cups water
8 cups water
1 medium onion, sliced and separated into rings
1½ teaspoons instant chicken bouillon granules
2 cloves garlic, minced
2 medium potatoes, sliced
2 medium carrots, cut into julienne pieces
2 small zucchini, sliced thin
½ cup elbow macaroni, uncooked
¼ cup oatmeal
¼ cup lemon juice
1 cup spinach leaves, snipped
1 cup watercress, snipped
Lemon slices (optional)

Rinse and dry garbanzo and kidney beans. In a 4-qt. Dutch oven or kettle, combine dry beans and 3 cups water. Bring to a boil and boil 2 minutes. Remove from heat. Cover; let stand 1 hour. Alternatively, soak beans in water overnight in a covered pan. Drain beans.

In the same Dutch oven, combine beans, 8 cups water, onion, bouillon granules, and garlic. Bring to a boil; reduce heat. Cover and simmer 1 hour.

In a small covered saucepan, cook potatoes in a small amount of water about 15 minutes or until very tender. Cool. Transfer undrained potatoes to a blender container or food processor bowl. Cover; blend or process till smooth.

Stir pureed potatoes, carrots, zucchini, macaroni, and oatmeal into bean mixture. Simmer 15 to 20 minutes or until vegetables and oatmeal are tender. Stir in lemon juice. Add snipped spinach and watercress. Top each serving with a lemon slice. Serves 6.

PER SERVING:
Cholesterol (mg): 0
Fat (grams): total 1; saturated 0
Exchanges: milk 0; fruit 0; bread/starch 1;
vegetable 2; meat 0; fat 0
Calories: 137

Vegetable-Stuffed Pitas
Serve with soup for a light supper

2 cups red leaf lettuce, shredded
¾ cup zucchini, thinly sliced
½ cup fresh mushrooms, sliced
½ cup red and green bell pepper, chopped
¼ cup red onion, chopped
1 tomato, chopped
1 cucumber, chopped
⅓ cup part-skim mozzarella cheese, shredded
3 tablespoons fresh oregano, minced and
    divided
½ cup plain low-fat yogurt
¼ teaspoon pepper
2 6-in. whole-wheat pita bread rounds

Combine first 8 ingredients in a medium bowl; add
2 tablespoons oregano, tossing gently. Set aside. Combine
remaining oregano, yogurt, and peppers; stir well.

Spread 2 tablespoons yogurt mixture inside each pita
half. Spoon 1 cup vegetable mixture into each bread
pocket. Serve immediately. Serves 4.

PER SERVING:
Cholesterol (mg): 10
Fat (grams): total 3; saturated 2
Exchanges: milk 0; fruit 0; bread/starch 1;
vegetable 1; meat 1; fat 0
Calories: 146

Fresh Vegetable Quiche

2 cups long-grain white rice, cooked
Egg substitute equal to 1 egg, lightly beaten
¾ cup (3 ozs.) Lorraine cheese, shredded,
   divided
¼ teaspoon salt
Vegetable cooking spray
1 cup fresh broccoli, chopped
1 cup fresh cauliflower, chopped
½ cup carrot, finely shredded
½ cup onion, finely shredded
¼ teaspoon salt
Egg substitute equal to 2 eggs, slightly beaten
¾ cup evaporated skim milk
¼ cup water
1 tablespoon fresh chives, minced
1 tablespoon fresh oregano
Pepper to taste

Combine rice, egg substitute, ¼ cup cheese, and salt in small bowl; stir well. Press mixture into a 9-in. pie plate coated with cooking spray. Bake at 350° for 5 minutes. Set aside

Place chopped broccoli and cauliflower in vegetable steamer over boiling water; cover and steam 5 minutes or until crisp-tender. Drain. Arrange broccoli, cauliflower, carrot, and onion in rice pie shell. Sprinkle with remaining ½ cup cheese.

Combine salt, egg substitute, and last 5 ingredients in small bowl, stir well; pour over cheese. Bake at 375° for 40 minutes or until set. Set stand 5 minutes. Serve warm. Serves 6.

PER SERVING:
Cholesterol (mg): 14
Fat (grams): total 3; saturated 2
Exchanges: milk 0; fruit 0; bread/starch 1;
vegetable 0; meat 1; fat 0
Calories: 150

✳ *Vegetarian Chili*

1 cup kidney beans (dry)
1 cup canned garbanzo beans
1 onion, diced
1 large carrot, diced
1 large stalk celery, diced
1 cup mushrooms, sliced
½ green bell pepper, diced
2 cloves garlic, minced
¾ cup tomato puree
2 large tomatoes, peeled and seeded
1 teaspoon (or to taste) cumin, ground
1½ teaspoons (or to taste) chili powder
½ teaspoon pepper

Place beans in saucepan and cover with water. Bring to boil. Boil 2 minutes and remove from heat. Cover and let stand 1 hour. Drain and place in large heavy saucepan. Add 4 cups water and cook until almost done.

Saute onion, carrot, celery, mushrooms, and green pepper in non-stick skillet. Add garlic, and saute a few seconds. Add tomato puree, tomatoes, cumin, chili powder, pepper, and sauteed vegetable mixture to beans. Simmer 40 minutes, adding water as needed to keep moist. Makes 5 (¾-cup) servings.

PER SERVING:
Cholesterol (mg): 0
Fat (grams): total 1; saturated 0
Exchanges: milk 0; fruit 0; bread/starch 2; vegetable 0; meat 1; fat 0
Calories: 197

Potato Latkes

6 medium potatoes, washed thoroughly, cubed
½ medium onion
3 tablespoons chives, minced
3 tablespoons flour
½ cup egg substitute
½ teaspoon salt (or to taste)
¼ teaspoon pepper, freshly ground
Safflower oil for frying

Put ¼ of every ingredient, except oil, in food processor and process until mixture is coarsely grated. Transfer to large bowl.

Repeat, processing ingredients ¼ at a time, until all ingredients are combined. Work quickly so mixture does not darken. Use at once.

Pour just enough safflower oil to cover bottom of electric fry pan or griddle evenly. Heat to 350°. Use ¼-cup measure to pour potato batter into heated pan. Fry each latke until crisp and brown, 2–3 minutes, then flip over and fry other side until brown. Drain latkes on paper towels to remove excess oil, put on a platter, and keep warm in a 200° oven until all batter has been fried. Serves 6.

PER SERVING:
Cholesterol (mg): less than 1
Fat (grams): total 3; saturated less than 1
Exchanges: milk 0; fruit 0; bread/starch 1½;
vegetable 0; meat 0; fat 0
Calories: 131

Zucchini and Cheese Latkes

2 lbs. small zucchini
1 medium potato, peeled
1 tablespoon lemon juice
1 cup green onions, sliced
¼ cup pimiento, chopped
½ cup Lorraine cheese, grated
2 cloves garlic, minced
   Egg substitute equal to 1 egg, beaten
1 cup flour
1 tablespoon sugar
½ teaspoon each, salt and pepper
   Vegetable oil for frying
   Mock Sour Cream (pg. 214) or applesauce, if
   desired

Grate zucchini and potato; remove as much water as possible by squeezing mixture with a towel. Put vegetables in large bowl and toss with lemon juice, green onions, pimiento, cheese, garlic, and egg substitute. Sift together flour, sugar, salt, and pepper. Blend into vegetable mixture.

Heat ¼ in. oil in large skillet until hot. Drop mixture by heaping tablespoons into hot oil and flatten with the back of a spoon. Fry until golden on both sides. Remove from skillet and place on paper towels to drain. Serve with mock sour cream or applesauce. Makes about 30 latkes. Serves 6.

PER SERVING:
Cholesterol (mg): 9
Fat (grams): total 3; saturated 2
Exchanges: milk 0; fruit 0; bread/starch 2;
vegetable 0; meat 0; fat 0
Calories: 187. Add 26 calories per serving with
applesauce, 30 calories with mock sour cream

Zucchini and Eggplant Casserole

2 small zucchinis, about ¾ lb.

2 small eggplants, about ¾ lb.

4 tablespoons olive oil

1 clove garlic, finely chopped

1 cup green onions, coarsely chopped

3 tablespoons chives, minced

4 plum tomatoes, about ¾ lb., cut into ¼ in. slices

1 teaspoon thyme

1 bay leaf

1 teaspoon rosemary

1 teaspoon basil

½ cup fresh parsley, coarsely chopped

Trim ends of zucchinis; do not peel. Cut into ⅜-in. cubes. This should result in about 4 cups. Trim ends of eggplants; do not peel. Cut into 3/8-in. cubes. This should result in about 4 cups.

In a heavy casserole, heat oil. When it is very hot, add zucchini and eggplant. Cook, stirring, about 4 minutes. Add garlic, onions, and chives. Cook, stirring, about 5 minutes. Add tomatoes, thyme, bay leaf, rosemary, and basil. Stir well and cook over medium heat 10 minutes, stirring often. Remove bay leaf and check seasoning. Garnish with parsley and serve immediately. Serves 4.

PER SERVING:

Cholesterol (mg): 0

Fat (grams): total 14; saturated 2

Exchanges: milk 0; fruit 0; bread/starch 1; vegetable 1; meat 0; fat 3

Calories: 233

*
Stuffed Zucchini

3 medium zucchinis
2 tablespoons margarine
1 clove garlic, minced
½ cup onion, chopped
¼ cup parsley, chopped
1 cup fresh mushrooms, chopped
2 tablespoons all-purpose flour
¼ teaspoon dried oregano, crushed
1 cup (4 oz.) low-cholesterol Monterey Jack
   cheese, shredded
2 tablespoons pimiento, chopped
¼ cup Parmesan cheese, freshly grated

Cook whole zucchini in boiling, salted water about 10 minutes or until tender. Drain. Cut in half lengthwise. Scoop out centers leaving ¼-in. shell; chop scooped-out vegetable and set aside.

Melt margarine in large skillet and saute garlic, onions, and parsley. Add mushrooms and continue cooking about 3 minutes or until tender. Stir in flour and oregano; remove from heat. Stir in Monterey Jack cheese and pimiento; stir in reserved chopped zucchini. Heat mixture through.

Preheat broiler. Fill zucchini shells, using approximately ¼ cup filling for each. Sprinkle with Parmesan cheese. Broil several inches from source of heat 3–5 minutes or until hot and bubbly. Serves 6.

Note: Stuffed zucchini may be assembled in advance, covered, and refrigerated up to 4 hours. Broil 5–7 minutes instead of 3 to 5.

PER SERVING:
Cholesterol (mg): 4
Fat (grams): total 9; saturated 2
Exchanges: milk 0; fruit 0; bread/starch 0;
vegetable 2; meat 1; fat 9
Calories: 145

✳ *Vegetarian Pizza*

CRUST

1 ¼-oz. pkg. active dry yeast
1 cup lukewarm water, 110°–115°
3 cups whole-wheat flour
1 tablespoon olive oil
½ teaspoon salt

TOPPING

2 cups Ultra Chic Marinara Sauce (pg. 213)
1 medium onion, sliced, about 2 cups
½ lb. mushrooms, thinly sliced, about 2 cups
1 small green bell pepper, sliced, about 1 cup
1 small red bell pepper, sliced, about 1 cup
2 small zucchinis, thinly sliced, about 2 cups
12 ozs. part-skim mozzarella cheese, sliced

Crust: Sprinkle yeast over water in large bowl. Stir to dissolve and let stand a few minutes in a warm place until bubbly. Add half the flour and mix well. Add olive oil and salt and stir until well mixed. Add 1 more cup flour and mix well.

Turn out onto floured board and knead, adding more flour as needed until smooth and elastic; 10 to 15 minutes. Put in oiled bowl and turn dough so that oiled side is up. Cover with waxed paper or plastic wrap. Put in warm place for 1½–2 hours or until dough is doubled in bulk. Punch down. Refrigerate until cold.

Divide dough into 2 balls and roll out on lightly floured board. Place each crust in a 12-in. pizza pan. Wrap and freeze if you are not going to use immediately. Thaw completely before placing sauce, toppings, and cheese on crust.

Topping: Make Marinara Sauce. Heat oven to 425°. Place 1 cup sauce on each pizza crust, spreading evenly. Arrange sliced onion, mushrooms, peppers, and zucchini decoratively on top of sauce. Bake for 10 minutes on lowest shelf of oven. Put cheese slices on pizza and bake another 15 minutes. Allow to stand 3–5 minutes before slicing. If pizza begins to brown too much before crust is done, place a square of aluminum foil lightly over top and continue to bake until bottom crust is lightly browned. Cut into 6 wedges. Serves 6.

PER SERVING:
Cholesterol (mg): 35
Fat (grams): total 19; saturated 8
Exchanges: milk 0; fruit 0; bread/starch 4;
vegetable 0; meat 2; fat 2
Calories: 515

Summer Pizza Sandwich
Serve these with a crisp green salad or fresh fruit salad for a delightful lunch or light supper

3 bagels
1 cup Ultra Chic Marinara Sauce (pg. 213)
1 tablespoon fresh basil, minced
1 tablespoon fresh oregano, minced (or 1 teaspoon dried)
½ teaspoon fresh garlic, minced
1 large ripe tomato, cut into 6 slices
6 thin slices part-skim mozzarella cheese
Olive oil

Heat broiler. Cut bagels crosswise in half. Toast or broil until golden. Mix pizza sauce, basil, oregano, and garlic in small bowl. Spread sauce evenly over toasted bagel halves. Top with tomato slice and cheese slice. Drizzle lightly with olive oil. Broil until cheese is golden. Serves 3.

PER SERVING:
Cholesterol (mg): 34
Fat (grams): total 21; saturated 8
Exchanges: milk 0; fruit 0; bread/starch 2;
vegetable 2; meat 2; fat 3
Calories: 460

Vegetables

Growing up in a French home has given me great respect for vegetables. Beautiful vegetables in every color imaginable offer a wide variety of different tastes. Vegetables have become an important part of American meals as cooks discover their versatility. No longer are vegetables only served with the life boiled out of them; they now appear with tantalizing sauces, spices, mushrooms, and magnificent herbs.

A low-cholesterol diet will benefit from the addition of special vegetable dishes since most vegetables do not contain any cholesterol. You may wish to consider an evening meal of only vegetables. This can be a most enjoyable dinner, and one that contains no fat—great for both the heart and the waistline.

Many of these vegetable dishes have been in my family for generations. No matter what you choose for your entree, you can add new dimensions to your meals with this collection of favorite vegetable recipes.

Baked Acorn Squash

2 acorn squash
2 teaspoons brown sugar
¼ teaspoon cinnamon
4 teaspoons margarine
4 teaspoons dry sherry

Cut each squash in half lengthwise. Place halves, cut side down, in a shallow baking pan. Cover bottom of pan with water. Bake squash at 400° for 50–60 minutes or until tender. Turn over. Fill each cavity with brown sugar, cinnamon, margarine, and 1 teaspoon sherry. Continue baking 15–20 minutes. Serves 4.

PER SERVING:
Cholesterol (mg): 0
Fat (grams): total 4; saturated less than 1
Exchanges: milk 0; fruit 0; bread/starch 1;
vegetable 1; meat 0; fat 1
Calories: 154

Confetti Corn Casserole

2 tablespoons melted margarine
1 teaspoon flour
¼ teaspoon dry mustard
2 teaspoons dried chives, chopped
1 teaspoon dried onions, chopped
1 teaspoon parsley flakes
2 cups whole kernel corn, drained
½ cup pimiento, chopped
½ cup whipped low-fat cottage cheese
½ cup low-fat yogurt

Blend margarine with flour until smooth. Add seasonings, drained corn, pimientos, cottage cheese, and yogurt. Mix well and pour into 1½-quart casserole. Bake at 325° for 25–30 minutes or until heated through. Serves 6.

PER SERVING:
Cholesterol (mg): 1
Fat (grams): total 5; saturated less than 1
Exchanges: milk 0; fruit 0; bread/starch 1;
vegetable 0; meat 0; fat 1
Calories: 126

Twice Baked Potatoes

4 medium potatoes, baked
1 cup low-fat cottage cheese
½ cup skim milk
1 cup green onions, chopped
1 tablespoon dried chives, minced
1 tablespoon Spike
  Freshly ground black pepper to taste
  Dash paprika
4 tablespoons fresh parsley, chopped

Cut potatoes in half lengthwise. Scoop out, leaving

shells intact for restuffing. Using a hand mixer, whip potatoes with cottage cheese, milk, onion, chives, Spike, and black pepper. Spoon mixture back into potato shells. Sprinkle with paprika and parsley. Bake 10 minutes at 350° or until just golden. Serves 8.

PER SERVING:
Cholesterol (mg): 1
Fat (grams): total less than 1; saturated less than 1
Exchanges: milk 0; fruit 0; bread/starch 1;
vegetable 0; meat 0; fat 0
Calories: 76

Golden Spaghetti Squash
A real show-stopper—perfect with chicken or fish

    1 (2½–3 lb.) spaghetti squash
    ½ cup margarine, at room temperature
    2 tablespoons brown sugar
    ¼ teaspoon ground cinnamon
    ¼ cup raisins
    1 orange, peeled and chopped

Preheat oven to 375°. Cut squash in half lengthwise. Using a spoon, scrape out seeds and loose stringy portion. Place squash halves, cut side down, on a shallow baking pan. Bake 35–45 minutes or until tender. While baking squash, combine margarine, brown sugar, cinnamon, and raisins in a small bowl. Invert baked squash shells. Using a fork, pull spaghetti-like strands up. Add half the raisin mixture to each cooked squash half. Lightly toss with a fork. Top with orange pieces. Serve warm. Serves 6 to 8.

PER SERVING:
Cholesterol (mg): 0
Fat (grams): total 11; saturated 2
Exchanges: milk 0; fruit 0; bread/starch 1;
vegetable 0; meat 0; fat 2
Calories: 162

Peas French Style

2 tablespoons margarine
6 spring onions, sliced
6 lettuce leaves, shredded finely
¼ teaspoon freshly ground black pepper
1 sprig each parsley and mint
1 teaspoon sugar
1 lb. shelled peas
1 cup water
1 teaspoon plain all-purpose flour
2 teaspoons margarine

Melt margarine in large saucepan, add spring onions, lettuce, pepper, parsley, mint, sugar, and peas. Stir in 1 cup water, bring to a boil, cover, and simmer gently about 20 minutes or until peas are very tender.

Remove and discard parsley and mint. Cream flour and margarine together thoroughly and add to peas in small amounts. Stir gently with a wooden spoon and heat gently until any remaining liquid is thickened. Serve hot. Serves 4.

PER SERVING:
Cholesterol (mg): 0
Fat (grams): total 8; saturated 1
Exchanges: milk 0; fruit 0; bread/starch 2;
vegetable 0; meat 0; fat 2
Calories: 430

Ratatouille Extraordinaire

2 cups onions, thinly sliced
2 cups red bell peppers in large chunks
4 cloves garlic, finely chopped
¾ cup olive oil, or as needed
4 cups zucchini, sliced
4 cups eggplant in chunks
2 cups mushrooms, sliced
2 teaspoons thyme
2 teaspoons Spike
   Freshly ground pepper to taste
1½ cups tomato puree

In large kettle, saute onions, red pepper, and garlic in oil until softened. Transfer mixture to a large casserole. Saute zucchini, eggplant, and mushrooms. Add to casserole. Season with herbs and pepper. Stir in tomato puree, mixing well. Bake in preheated 400° oven for 30 minutes. Serves 12.

PER SERVING:
Cholesterol (mg): 0
Fat (grams): total 14; saturated 2
Exchanges: milk 0; fruit 0; bread/starch 0;
vegetable 2; meat 0; fat 3
Calories: 180

✳ Italian Style Zucchini

2 lbs. zucchini, sliced thinly
4 tablespoons onion, chopped
1 cup stewed Italian tomatoes
½ teaspoon oregano
1 tablespoon cornstarch
4 tablespoons water
½ cup Parmesan cheese, freshly grated

Place zucchini, onion, and stewed tomatoes in a medium saucepan. Cook on medium-high heat 15 minutes. Lower heat and add oregano. Mix cornstarch with water and stir into vegetable mixture. Cook another 10 minutes on low heat. Remove from heat and stir in Parmesan cheese. Serves 6.

PER SERVING:
Cholesterol (mg): total 3; saturated 1
Exchanges: milk 0; fruit 0; bread/starch 0;
vegetable 2; meat 0; fat 0
Calories: 60

✳ Stir-Fried Asparagus

2 lbs. fresh asparagus spears
2 tablespoons margarine
1 tablespoon olive oil
1 tablespoon Tamari soy sauce
1 teaspoon lemon juice
¼ cup chicken stock (p. 43)
⅛ teaspoon white pepper
2 tablespoons pimiento, diced

Cut off about 2 inches of the tough end of each asparagus spear. Cut spears diagonally into ¼-in. slices. Heat margarine and oil in a medium skillet; add asparagus slices.

Cook, stirring over medium-high heat, about 2 minutes. Stir in soy sauce, lemon juice, stock, and pepper. Cover and cook another 2–3 minutes or until tender. Sprinkle with pimiento. Serves 6.

PER SERVING:
Cholesterol (mg): 0
Fat (grams): total 6; saturated 1
Exchanges: milk 0; fruit 0; bread/starch 0; vegetable 1; meat 0; fat 1
Calories: 95

Mushrooms Normandy

2 lbs. mushrooms, sliced
1 teaspoon lemon juice
1 small onion, finely chopped
1 clove garlic, minced
2 tablespoons fine breadcrumbs
2 tablespoons chives, minced
1 tablespoon pimientos, minced
   Freshly ground pepper to taste
1 tablespoon parsley, finely chopped

In a large skillet, saute mushrooms over low heat 3 minutes. Stir in lemon juice. Add onion, garlic, and breadcrumbs. Saute over high heat 3 minutes. Add chives and pimientos. Mix well and sprinkle with parsley and pepper to taste. Serve immediately. Serves 6.

PER SERVING:
Cholesterol (mg): 0
Fat (grams): total 1; saturated less than 1
Exchanges: milk 0; fruit 0; bread/starch 0; vegetable 2; meat 0; fat 0
Calories: 64

✳ *Crispy Potato Skins*

4 baking potatoes
2 tablespoons margarine, melted
1 teaspoon Spike
  Dash pepper
1 cup Parmesan cheese, freshly grated
⅓ cup green onions, chopped
2 tablespoons imitation bacon chips
¼ cup mock sour cream, if desired

Preheat oven to 425°. Scrub and dry potatoes. Bake 60 minutes or until soft. Cool enough to handle. Cut each potato in half lengthwise. With a spoon, scoop out pulp, leaving a ⅛-in. shell. Set potato pulp aside for another use.

Place potato shells, skin side down, in a 13x9-in. baking pan. Brush inside of shells with melted margarine. Sprinkle with Spike and pepper. Bake 10 minutes. Remove from oven; set aside. In a small bowl, combine cheese, green onions, and bacon chips. Toss cheese mixture lightly. Spread about 2 tablespoons cheese mixture in each potato skin. Change oven setting to broil. Broil potato skins, 3–4 inches below heat, 1–1½ minutes or until bubbly. Serve hot with mock sour cream (pg. 214) if desired. Serves 2.

PER SERVING:
Cholesterol (mg): 13
Fat (grams): total 17; saturated 5
Exchanges: milk 0; fruit 0; bread/starch 3;
vegetable 0; meat 1; fat 3
Calories: 402

Spinach-Stuffed Mushrooms
I like to serve these surrounding a roast chicken or as an appetizer

1 10-oz. pkg. frozen chopped spinach or 1
  bunch fresh spinach
14 to 16 large mushrooms

2 tablespoons margarine
1 garlic clove, crushed
1 teaspoon Worcestershire sauce
½ cup breadcrumbs
1 teaspoon prepared mustard
⅛ teaspoon pepper
2 tablespoons low-cal mayonnaise
¼ cup Parmesan cheese, grated

Cook frozen spinach according to package directions. If using fresh spinach, place spinach and small amount of water in a medium saucepan. Cook over medium heat 2–5 minutes. Drain cooked spinach and press out excess water with the back of a wooden spoon; set aside.

Remove stems from mushrooms and chop well. In a medium skillet, melt margarine. Add chopped mushroom stems and garlic. Saute until stems are soft; remove from heat. Add Worcestershire sauce, breadcrumbs, mustard, pepper, mayonnaise, and cheese. Stir in drained cooked spinach.

Preheat oven to 350°. Spoon some spinach mixture into each mushroom cap. Place mushrooms, stuffed side up, in an 11x7-in. baking pan. Pour ¾ cup of water in bottom of pan, being careful not to pour water on mushrooms. Bake 20 minutes or until mushrooms are hot. Remove baked mushrooms from pan and discard any remaining liquid. Serves 7 or 8 (2 mushrooms each).

PER SERVING:
Cholesterol (mg): 2
Fat (grams): total 5; saturated 1
Exchanges: milk 0; fruit 0; bread/starch 0;
vegetable 2; meat 0; fat 1
Calories: 88

Tomatoes Stuffed with Mushrooms and Cheese

4 large fresh tomatoes
1 lb. fresh mushrooms, diced
1 medium-size onion, chopped
1 green bell pepper, chopped
3 cloves garlic, crushed
2 tablespoons olive oil
½ teaspoon oregano
½ cup black olives, diced
½ cup parsley, chopped
¼ teaspoon cayenne pepper
½ cup Parmesan cheese, freshly grated

Preheat oven to 350°. Scoop out center of tomatoes and put aside in a small dish. In a large frying pan, saute mushrooms, onion, pepper, and garlic in olive oil over medium heat for 10 minutes. Add tomato pulp, oregano, olives, parsley, and cayenne pepper; stir and cook together 5 minutes.

Place tomato shells in an oiled baking dish, and fill each shell with sauteed mixture. Sprinkle each with Parmesan cheese and bake 10 minutes. Serves 4.

PER SERVING:
Cholesterol (mg): 10
Fat (grams): total 17; saturated 1
Exchanges: milk 0; fruit 0; bread/starch 0;
vegetable 3; meat 1; fat 3
Calories: 262

Asparagus with Mustard Cream Sauce

ASPARAGUS

2½ lbs. fresh asparagus, trimmed

MUSTARD CREAM SAUCE

  2 tablespoons margarine

  3 tablespoons all-purpose flour

  1 cup chicken broth, made from 1 chicken
    bouillon cube

  1 cup skim milk

  ¼ cup Dijon-style mustard

  1 teaspoon lemon juice

    Dash white pepper

Mustard Cream Sauce (make first): Melt margarine in medium-size saucepan. Stir in flour and cook 1 minute. Add chicken broth and skim milk, stirring constantly with a whisk. Bring to a boil. Lower heat and simmer 5 minutes, stirring occasionally. Remove from heat and whisk in mustard, lemon juice, and white pepper. Keep warm while cooking asparagus; do not let boil.

Asparagus: Bring to a boil 2 quarts water in large skillet or Dutch oven. Add asparagus. Cook 3–5 minutes or until tender-crisp. Drain in a colander. Arrange on a serving platter. Pour Mustard Cream Sauce over asparagus and serve. Serves 8.

> *PER SERVING:*
> *Cholesterol (mg): less than 1*
> *Fat (grams): total 4; saturated less than 1*
> *Exchanges: milk 0; fruit 0; bread/starch 0;*
> *vegetable 1; meat 0; fat 1*
> *Calories: 81*

Potato Pie

**When the occasion calls for a light supper, just
add a salad and crusty French bread**

> Egg substitute equivalent to 2 eggs
> 2 cups mashed potatoes
> 1 cup onions, finely chopped
> 1 cup Lorraine cheese, grated
> 1½ cups low-fat cottage cheese
> ⅓ cup green onions, chopped
> ¼ cup Parmesan cheese, grated
> ¼ teaspoon white pepper

Preheat oven to 350°. Grease a 10-in., deep-dish pie plate with vegetable spray; set aside. In a large bowl, mix all ingredients until well blended. Pour into pie plate. Bake 70 minutes or until filling is puffed and evenly brown on top. Serves 6.

PER SERVING:
Cholesterol (mg): 22
Fat (grams): total 8; saturated 4
Exchanges: milk 0; fruit 0; bread/starch 1;
vegetable 0; meat 2; fat 0
Calories: 205

Garlic Mashed Potatoes

> 6 large new potatoes
> ½ cup skim milk, heated
> 4 tablespoons margarine
> 4 cloves garlic, finely minced
> ½ cup fresh chives, minced

Boil potatoes in jackets until tender. Remove from heat and place in cold water. Remove skins and "rice" them while still warm. Add heated skim milk and margarine. Whip the potatoes with a hand mixer. Add garlic and whip again. Place potatoes in a bowl, top with chives, and blend chives throughout the potatoes. Serve hot or cold as an appetizer. Serves 4.

PER SERVING:
Cholesterol (mg): 1
Fat (grams): total 5; saturated 2
Exchanges: milk 0; fruit 0; bread/starch 2;
vegetable 1; meat 0; fat 1
Calories: 233

Bayou Mashed Potatoes

6 large new potatoes
½ cup skim milk, heated
4 tablespoons margarine
3 tablespoons horseradish

Boil potatoes in jackets until tender. Remove from heat and place in cold water. Remove skins and "rice" them while still warm. Add heated skim milk, margarine, and horseradish. Whip until fluffy. Serve hot or cold as an appetizer. Serves 4.

PER SERVING:
Cholesterol (mg): 1
Fat (grams): total 11; saturated 2
Exchanges: milk 0; fruit 0; bread/starch 2;
vegetable 1; meat 0; fat 1
Calories: 238

*
Broccoli Casserole

3 10-oz. pkgs. frozen chopped broccoli
6 tablespoons margarine
4 tablespoons flour
1 cup chicken broth
2 cups skim milk
⅔ cup water
2 cups Pepperidge Farm stuffing mix

Cook broccoli according to package directions until tender-crisp. Drain well and place in an oiled, 2-quart casserole.

Melt 2 tablespoons margarine in a saucepan. Stir in flour and cook briefly. Add chicken broth and milk and cook, stirring constantly, until thickened. Set aside.

Melt remaining 4 tablespoons of margarine in the water. Mix with stuffing. Pour chicken broth sauce over broccoli; sprinkle with stuffing mixture and bake at 400° for 20 minutes or until crusty on top. Serves 6.

PER SERVING:
Cholesterol (mg): 16
Fat (grams): total 18; saturated 3
Exchanges: milk 0; fruit 0; bread/starch 1;
vegetable 2; meat 1; fat 3
Calories: 311

Sauces

Divine sauces are used to enhance the taste of a dish and to lend excitement to its presentation. A sauce should complement the meal but never overpower it. A low-cholesterol meal can be made special with the addition of the right sauce.

A good sauce is light and made with fresh, natural ingredients such as herbs, spices, vegetables, wines, lemon juice, onions, and garlic. Sauces for a low-cholesterol diet should not contain heavy cream, butter, or sour cream.

In this section you will find a selection of sauces, including Italian sauces, trendy sauces, my creations, and, I hope, some ideas for you to develop into your own creations.

Alicia's Holiday Cranberry Sauce for Fowl

This recipe comes from my friend Alicia, and it is very special

1 pkg. cranberries
3 ripe pears, peeled
1 cup sugar
2 splashes white wine
½ cup cranberry juice

Combine all ingredients in blender and mix until smooth. The sauce should be gravy texture. Serve with all your holiday turkeys and poultry. Makes 1 cup.

PER SERVING (two tablespoons):
Cholesterol (mg): 0
Fat (grams): total 0; saturated 0
Exchanges: milk 0; fruit 2; bread/starch 0;
vegetable 0; meat 0; fat 0
Calories: 145

Basic White Sauce I

3 tablespoons margarine
6 tablespoons whole-wheat flour
3 cups skim milk

In a saucepan, melt the margarine and stir until golden brown. Stir in the flour until crumbly. Whisk in milk. Stir over medium heat, beating with a whisk until thickened. Use as directed in recipe. Makes 3 cups.

PER SERVING (two tablespoons):
Cholesterol (mg): 1
Fat (grams): total 1; saturated 0
Exchanges: milk 0; fruit 0; bread/starch ½;
vegetable 0; meat 0; fat 0
Calories: 40

Basic White Sauce II

4 tablespoons margarine
4 tablespoons whole-wheat flour
8 tablespoons non-fat dry milk
1 cup water

Melt margarine and stir in flour. Add the non-fat dry milk and water. Place over low heat and cook, stirring constantly, until sauce is thick and smooth. Makes 2 cups.

Note: This recipe may also be made with skim milk or evaporated skim milk. You can add Molly McButter sprinkles or Molly McButter sour cream and chive sprinkles as well as other herbs and seasonings to add interesting flavors to this sauce.

PER SERVING (two tablespoons):
Cholesterol (mg): 0
Fat (grams): total 3; saturated 0
Exchanges: milk 0; fruit 0; bread/starch 0;
vegetable 0; meat 0; fat 1
Calories: 45

Dill Sauce

1½ cups low-fat yogurt
   Sugar, pinch
 4 teaspoons lemon juice
 1 teaspoon onion, grated
 1 clove garlic, minced
 2 tablespoons fresh dill, chopped well; or 1
   tablespoon dill weed

Place the yogurt in a small bowl and add rest of ingredients. Mix well and refrigerate until ready to use. Makes 1½ cups.

PER SERVING:
Calories: 16 per two-tablespoon serving

Mock Hollandaise Sauce

¼ cup Mock Sour Cream (pg. 214)
¼ cup plain low-fat yogurt
1 teaspoon lemon juice
½ teaspoon prepared mustard

In small saucepan, combine all ingredients. Cook and stir over very low heat until heated through; do not boil. Serve over poultry and cooked vegetables. Makes ½ cup.

PER SERVING:
Calories: 13 per one-tablespoon serving

Sangria Sundae Sauce

This sauce is delicious over angel food cake or with frozen yogurt

1 8¼-oz. can pineapple chunks; or fresh pineapple
1 tablespoon cornstarch
½ cup dry red wine
2 tablespoons frozen lemonade concentrate
2 oranges, peeled and sectioned
2 fresh peaches, peeled and sliced

Drain pineapple, reserving syrup. In a small saucepan, stir reserved syrup into cornstarch. Add wine and lemonade concentrate. Cook and stir over medium heat until mixture thickens and bubbles. Stir in pineapple chunks, orange sections, and peach slices. Serve warm or cold over angel food cake or ice milk. Makes two cups.

PER SERVING (two tablespoons):
Cholesterol (mg): 0
Fat (grams): total 0; saturated 0

Exchanges: milk 0; fruit 1; bread/starch 0;
vegetable 0; meat 0; fat 0
Calories: 51

Hot Fudge Sauce

¾ **cup sugar**
½ **cup Dutch cocoa**
1 **5-oz. can evaporated skim milk**
⅓ **cup light corn syrup**
⅓ **cup margarine**
1 **teaspoon vanilla**

Combine sugar and cocoa in small saucepan; blend
in evaporated milk and corn syrup. Cook over medium
heat, stirring constantly, until mixture boils; boil and stir
1 minute. Remove from heat; stir in margarine and vanilla.
Serve warm. Makes 1 cup.

PER SERVING (two tablespoons):
Cholesterol (mg): 0
Fat (grams): total 8; saturated 1
Exchanges: milk 0; fruit 0; bread/starch 2;
vegetable 0; meat 0; fat 1
Calories: 216

Ultra Chic Marinara Sauce*
A basic pasta sauce, I usually make 4 times the
recipe and store it in 2-cup measurements

2 **tablespoons olive oil**
5 **cloves garlic**
1 **medium onion, chopped**
1 **28-oz. can crushed tomatoes**

1 cup mushrooms, sliced
1 tablespoon fresh basil
1 tablespoon oregano
2 tablespoons parsley, chopped
½ cup Parmesan cheese, freshly grated

Place olive oil and garlic in large saucepan. Saute the garlic in the oil until garlic begins to brown. Remove garlic from oil with slotted spoon. Add onion to the oil and saute lightly.

Add tomatoes and mushrooms and cook on medium heat for about 30 minutes. Add basil, oregano, and parsley and bring to a boil. Remove from heat and stir in Parmesan cheese. Makes about 3½ cups sauce. Serves 4 over pasta.

*Note: I also use this for pizza sauce; just add a little more oregano.

PER SERVING:
Cholesterol (mg): 4
Fat (grams): total 9; saturated 2
Exchanges: milk 0; fruit 0; bread/starch 0;
vegetable 2; meat 0; fat 2
Calories: 148

Mock Sour Cream

2 tablespoons skim milk
1 tablespoon lemon juice
¼ cup low-fat yogurt
1 cup low-fat cottage cheese

Place all ingredients in blender and mix until smooth and creamy. Use in place of sour cream as a base for dips or add to hot dishes just before serving.

Desserts

A dessert masterpiece is often considered the crowning glory of an outstanding meal. Dessert often is the one part of a meal that hosts or hostesses will purchase away from home instead of preparing themselves. Yet there is no better way to draw compliments than to present a dessert, made from scratch, that you have created for the occasion. A low-cholesterol diet does not mean giving up desserts. It does mean, however, selecting healthy desserts such as those you'll find in this chapter.

A dessert should complement the meal that precedes it. Serve something light, such as an ice, mousse, or fresh fruit, if the main course has been substantial. When you have served a light meal, such as a salad or soup, offer a rich dessert—pie or cheesecake, for example.

The recipes that follow provide some outstanding suggestions for desserts of every description. You will find luscious pies, cakes, cookies, and special occasion desserts such as Amaretto cheesecake and brownies. You will discover desserts that take only a few minutes to make and others that take more time. You will find recipes that require no baking and some that are created in the refrigerator.

Desserts offer a cook a creative way to add excitement to a meal. Discover the pride of serving your family and friends mouthwatering temptations made especially for them.

*

Peach Blueberry Crisp

2 lbs. fresh peaches, peeled and sliced*
1 cup fresh blueberries
1 cup Bisquick baking mix
1 cup packed brown sugar
¾ teaspoon cinnamon, ground
¼ cup margarine, softened

Arrange sliced peaches and blueberries in an ungreased 8-in. square baking pan.

In a medium bowl, combine Bisquick, brown sugar, and cinnamon; mix well. Melt margarine in a small skillet or in your microwave and mix well with Bisquick mixture, stirring until it resembles coarse crumbs. Sprinkle this mixture over the fruit. Bake uncovered at 400° for 18–20 minutes. Serves 6.

*Note: You can substitute 1-lb. can of apple pie filling for the peaches if you wish a change.

PER SERVING:
Cholesterol (mg): 0
Fat (grams): total 10; saturated 1
Exchanges: milk 0; fruit 1; bread/starch 3;
vegetable 0; meat 0; fat 2
Calories: 369

Tortoni

⅓ cup flaked coconut, toasted*
¼ cup sugar
⅓ cup water
3 egg whites
    Salt, dash
¼ teaspoon almond extract
2 cups Mock Whipped Cream (pg. 238)
⅓ cup glace red cherries, chopped
⅓ cup almonds, blanched, chopped, and
    toasted*

In food processor, process coconut until it resembles texture of dry breadcrumbs. Line 12 medium muffin cups with paper liners.

In very small saucepan, combine sugar and water; bring to a boil over medium heat. Continue to cook until syrup reaches soft ball stage (232° on candy thermometer).

In large mixer bowl, combine egg whites and salt; beat at high speed until foamy. Add hot syrup in a fine steady stream, beating constantly. Beat in almond extract. Fold in mock whipped cream, then cherries and almonds. Spoon into muffin cups and sprinkle with coconut. Freeze until firm. Serves 12.

*Note: To toast coconut and almonds, bake in shallow pans in 350° oven, shaking pan occasionally, until golden, about 10 minutes for coconut, 10–15 minutes for almonds.

PER SERVING:
Cholesterol (mg): 0
Fat (grams): total 4; saturated 1
Exchanges: milk 0; fruit 0; bread/starch 1;
vegetable 0; meat 0; fat 1
Calories: 108

Pears Belle Helene

1 cup sugar
1¼ cups water
3 tablespoons honey
4 pears, fresh
1 recipe Hot Fudge Sauce (pg. 213)

Place sugar in a saucepan with water and heat gently, stirring until sugar is dissolved. Stir in honey. Peel, core, and halve pears. Cook halves gently in syrup for 15–20 minutes or until tender. Drain and cool. Place pears in 4 glass serving dishes. Pour Hot Fudge Sauce over pears. Serves 4.

PER SERVING (includes two tablespoons of hot fudge sauce):
Cholesterol (mg): 0
Fat (grams): total 8; saturated 1
Exchanges: milk 0; fruit 1; bread/starch 5; vegetable 0; meat 0; fat 1
Calories: 513

Melon Balls Supreme

2 cups cantaloupe balls
2 cups honeydew balls
2 cups watermelon balls
¾ cup orange juice
½ cup honey
2 tablespoons orange rind, grated fresh
2 tablespoons lime rind, grated fresh

Mix all melon balls in a large bowl. Divide among 4 dessert dishes so that each dish has an assortment of melons. Place orange juice and honey in a small bowl. Mix well. Pour over melon balls. Sprinkle orange and lime rind over melon balls. Serves 4.

PER SERVING:
Cholesterol (mg): 0
Fat (grams): total 0; saturated 0
Exchanges: milk 0; fruit 4; bread/starch 0;
vegetable 0; meat 0; fat 0
Calories: 235

Strawberries Barbara

4 cups strawberries, sliced
1 cup low-fat cottage cheese
2 tablespoons skim milk
6 tablespoons sugar
¼ cup low-fat yogurt
1 tablespoon orange juice
6 tablespoons orange peel, grated
2 teaspoons candied ginger, minced

Divide strawberries among 8, ½-cup dessert dishes. Place cottage cheese, skim milk, and sugar in blender. Process until smooth. Add yogurt and remaining ingredients except candied ginger. Blend until smooth. Stir in candied ginger. Top strawberries with sauce. Serves 8.

PER SERVING:
Cholesterol (mg): 1
Fat (grams): total 0; saturated 0
Exchanges: milk 0; fruit 1; bread/starch 0;
vegetable 0; meat 0; fat 0
Calories: 87

Carrot and Oatmeal Cookies
These cookies can be enjoyed for a breakfast on the run

⅔ cup margarine
⅔ cup sugar
1 teaspoon vanilla
¾ cup flour
½ teaspoon baking soda
½ teaspoon salt
1½ cup regular (not quick) rolled oats
1 cup carrots, shredded
½ cup wheat germ

Cream margarine, sugar, and vanilla. Sift flour, baking soda, and salt. Add to margarine and mix well. Add oats, carrots, and wheat germ and mix well. Drop by tablespoons on greased cookie sheet and bake at 350° for 12–14 minutes or until golden. Makes 3 dozen cookies

PER SERVING (one cookie):
Cholesterol (mg): 0
Fat (grams): total 4; saturated 1
Exchanges: milk 0; fruit 0; bread/starch ½;
vegetable 0; meat 0; fat 1
Calories: 77

Carrot and Peach Cookies

2 cups carrots, peeled and diced
¾ cup margarine, softened
½ cup sugar (or to taste)
1 large egg
1 teaspoon vanilla
¼ cup peach preserves
2 cups flour
2 teaspoons baking powder

½ teaspoon salt
Poppy seed (optional)

Cook carrots in salted water until tender. Drain and mash. Set aside.

Heat oven to 375°. Beat margarine and sugar in electric mixture until light and fluffy. Beat in egg and vanilla. Beat until well blended. Stir in mashed carrots. Add peach preserves and mix well.

Sift together flour, baking powder, and salt. Add to carrot mixture. Beat until blended. Drop from a teaspoon onto ungreased baking sheets. Top with poppy seed, if using. Bake 10–12 minutes. Cool on wire rack. Makes about 4 dozen cookies. Two cookies per serving.

PER SERVING (two cookies):
Cholesterol (mg): 12
Fat (grams): total 6; saturated 1
Exchanges: milk 0; fruit 0; bread/starch 1;
vegetable 0; meat 0; fat 1
Calories: 120

Parisian Sable Cookies

1 cup (2 sticks) margarine, room temperature
1 cup sugar
Egg substitute equal to 2 eggs
4 cups unbleached all-purpose flour
1 cup (or more) fruit-only preserves (such as strawberry, raspberry, apricot, or orange marmalade)
Powdered sugar

Using electric mixer, beat margarine until soft. Add sugar and beat until light and fluffy. Blend in egg substitute, scraping down sides of bowl. Add flour and mix until dough just comes together. Wrap in plastic and refrigerate until firm, at least 2 hours or overnight.

Preheat oven to 350°. Line baking sheets with parchment paper. Divide dough in half. Roll out 1 piece on lightly floured surface to ⅛-in. thickness. Cut four rounds, using 2½-in. round cutter. Gather scraps and refrigerate. Repeat rolling and cutting with remaining dough. Save scraps. Using small round cutter, cut out holes in half of the rounds. Save scraps. Combine all scraps together. Reroll and cut out additional rounds from scraps. Be sure to cut holes in only half of the rounds.

Arrange all rounds on prepared baking sheets. Bake until dough is set and edges are golden, 10–15 minutes. Cool completely on rack.

Spread thin layer of preserve on cookies without holes. Top with cookies with holes, pressing gently. If desired, spoon more preserve into holes. Dust with powdered sugar. Makes 40 sandwich cookies.

PER SERVING (one cookie):
Cholesterol (mg): 0
Fat (grams): total 5; saturated 1
Exchanges: milk 0; fruit 0; bread/starch 1;
vegetable 0; meat 0; fat 1
Calories: 122

Rum Raisin Cookies

1 cup raisins
½ cup warm rum (or 3 tablespoons rum extract in ½ cup warm water)
1 cup margarine, softened
½ cup powdered sugar, sifted
2 cups flour
¼ teaspoon salt
¼ teaspoon baking powder

Bring raisins to boil in rum. Remove from heat. Cover and let stand 30 minutes. Drain. Cream margarine and powdered sugar. Sift flour with salt and baking powder; add gradually to creamed mixture. Add raisins. Roll out dough to ½-in. thickness on floured board. Cut with cookie cutters. Bake at 375° for 20 minutes. Makes 12 cookies.

***PER SERVING** (one cookie):*
***Cholesterol (mg):** 0*
***Fat (grams):** total 15; saturated 3*
***Exchanges:** milk 0; fruit 0; bread/starch 2;*
vegetable 0; meat 0; fat 3
***Calories:** 276*

Crispy Chocolate Raisin Cookies

½ cup margarine
1 cup sugar
1 egg
1 teaspoon vanilla
1¼ cups all-purpose flour
½ teaspoon baking soda
¼ teaspoon salt
2 cups crisp rice cereal
1 6-oz. pkg. semisweet chocolate morsels
1 cup dark raisins

Cream margarine; gradually add sugar, beating until light and fluffy. Add egg and vanilla, beating well. Combine flour, soda, and salt; add to creamed mixture, beating well. Stir in the rice cereal, chocolate morsels, and raisins.

Drop dough in heaping teaspoonfuls onto lightly greased cookie sheets. Bake at 350° for 13 minutes. Cool slightly on cookie sheets; remove to wire racks. Makes 42 cookies.

***PER SERVING** (two cookies):*
***Cholesterol (mg):** 13*
***Fat (grams):** total 4; saturated 1*
***Exchanges:** milk 0; fruit 0; bread/starch 1;*
vegetable 0; meat 0; fat 1
***Calories:** 126*

Strawberry-Almond Shortcake

3 cups fresh strawberries, sliced
2 tablespoons sugar
1⅔ cups all-purpose flour
1 tablespoon sugar
2 teaspoons baking soda
1 teaspoon baking powder
3 tablespoons margarine
1 beaten egg
1 teaspoon almond extract
½ cup buttermilk or skim milk
Vegetable cooking spray
1 recipe Mock Whipped Cream (pg. 238)

Combine strawberries and 2 tablespoons sugar; refrigerate at least 1 hour.

In a medium bowl, stir together flour, the 1 tablespoon sugar, baking soda, and baking powder; cut in margarine till mixture resembles coarse crumbs. Combine egg, almond extract, and buttermilk; add to flour mixture all at once, stirring until mixed.

Spray an 8-in. round baking pan with non-stick cooking spray. With lightly floured hands, spread dough into pan. Bake in a 450° oven about 10 minutes or until golden. Cool.

Split in half; place bottom portion on a serving plate. Top with some of the berries. Place top portion over berries. Spread mock whipped cream over cake, and spoon on berries. Place several dollops of mock whipped cream over berries. Serves 8.

PER SERVING:
Cholesterol (mg): 36
Fat (grams): total 6; saturated 1
Exchanges: milk 0; fruit 1; bread/starch 1;
vegetable 0; meat 0; fat 1
Calories: 203

✳
Carrot Cake

CAKE

2 cups all-purpose flour
2 teaspoons baking soda
2 teaspoons cinnamon
½ teaspoon salt
6 egg whites
¾ cup corn oil
¾ cup buttermilk
2 cups sugar
2 teaspoons vanilla extract
¾ cup canned crushed pineapple, packed in
  juice, drained
2 cups carrots (about 4 carrots), peeled and grated
⅓ cup dark raisins

FROSTING

1 cup low-fat cottage cheese
3 tablespoons plain low-fat yogurt
3 tablespoons sugar
1 teaspoon vanilla extract

Cake: Preheat oven to 350°. Spray a 13x9-in. pan with non-stick vegetable cooking spray.

Sift flour, baking soda, cinnamon, and salt together.

Beat egg whites in a large bowl. Add oil, buttermilk, sugar, and vanilla. Mix well. Add flour mixture, pineapple, carrots, and raisins. Stir well. Pour into pan; bake until a toothpick inserted in center comes out clean, 45 to 50 minutes. Cool before frosting.

Frosting: Blend cheese, yogurt, sugar, and vanilla in a food processor or blender until smooth. Refrigerate in a tightly covered container until ready to frost the cake. Refrigerate cake after frosting. Serves 15.

PER SERVING:
Cholesterol (mg): 1
Fat (grams): total 11; saturated 1
Exchanges: milk 0; fruit 0; bread/starch 3;

vegetable 0; meat 0; fat 2
Calories: 313

Divine Chocolate Angel Food Cake with Raspberries

CAKE

1½ cups superfine sugar, divided
¾ cup cake flour
¼ cup cocoa
2 cups egg whites (about 16 large eggs)
1½ teaspoons cream of tartar
1 teaspoon vanilla
¼ teaspoon salt

GLAZE

8 ozs. semisweet chocolate
½ cup (1 stick) margarine
¼ cup water
1 cup fresh raspberries*

Cake: Place rack in center of oven and preheat to 375°. Set aside an ungreased 10-in. tube pan.

Divide sugar in half. Sift one-half with flour and cocoa three times. Set aside. Sift other half of sugar three times. Set aside.

Put egg whites in a large grease-free bowl and beat on low speed until they are foamy. Add cream of tartar, vanilla, and salt and gradually increase beating speed to medium. Slowly add the sifted sugar-only portion and continue to beat on medium speed until whites have increased in volume about fivefold and hold their shape but are still shiny and moist. Gently fold in sifted sugar-flour-cocoa mixture in thirds.

Transfer to tube pan. Smooth surface with a spatula and tap pan on counter three or four times to remove any air pockets. Bake about 30–35 minutes or until a toothpick inserted in center comes out clean. Invert cake over narrow-necked bottle to cool completely.

Glaze: Make glaze while cake is cooling. Melt chocolate with margarine and water in top of a double boiler over simmering water; cook about 2 minutes, stirring occasionally. Cool glaze until it is spreadable.

When cake is completely cool, loosen it from sides of pan with a knife and invert onto a rack. Frost with glaze and top with raspberries. Serves 10.

*Note: This cake can also be made with strawberries, if desired.

PER SERVING:
Cholesterol (mg): 0
Fat (grams): total 21; saturated 1
Exchanges: milk 0; fruit 1; bread/starch 2;
vegetable 0; meat 0; fat 4
Calories: 380

Lemon Sponge Cake

¾ cup matzo cake meal
1⅓ cups sugar, divided
12 large egg whites
¼ teaspoon salt
2 tablespoons lemon juice
2 tablespoons lemon rind, grated

Put rack in center of oven and preheat to 325°. Spray a 10-in. tube pan with vegetable cooking spray.

Sift matzo meal with ½ cup sugar and set aside.

Beat egg whites and salt in a large bowl until they hold soft peaks. Gradually add remaining sugar, beating well as you add it. Continue beating until whites are thick and glossy. Add juice and lemon rind. Gently but thoroughly, fold matzo-sugar mixture into whites. Transfer to pan and lightly tap pan on counter several times to settle batter.

Bake until golden, 50–60 minutes. Invert pan so cake is upside down and cool to room temperature. Loosen sides of cake from pan with a knife and invert onto plate. Serve plain with sifted powdered sugar or with fruit or sauce. Serves 10–12.

PER SERVING:
Cholesterol (mg): 0
Fat (grams): total 0; saturated 0
Exchanges: milk 0; fruit 0; bread/starch 2;
vegetable 0; meat 0; fat 0
Calories: 150

Brownies

½ cup water, boiling
½ cup unsweetened cocoa powder
1½ cups sugar
⅓ cup corn oil
1 teaspoon vanilla
4 egg whites, at room temperature
1¼ cups flour
1 teaspoon baking powder
¼ teaspoon salt

Preheat oven to 350°. Spray a 13x9-in. pan with vegetable cooking spray.

In a large bowl, combine boiling water and cocoa. Mix with a wire whisk until well blended and smooth. Add sugar, oil, vanilla, egg whites, flour, baking powder, and salt. Mix well with wire whisk. Pour into prepared pan.

Bake until wooden toothpick inserted in center comes out clean, about 25 minutes. Makes about 24 brownies.

PER SERVING: (one brownie)
Cholesterol (mg): 0
Fat (grams): total 3; saturated 0
Exchanges: milk 0; fruit 0; bread/starch 1;
vegetable 0; meat 0; fat 0
Calories: 101

Chocolate Cupcake Surprise
The surprise is a cherry filling!

1 cup vegetable shortening
2 cups sugar
1½ teaspoons vanilla
6 egg whites
1½ cups hot water
1¼ cups cocoa
3¾ cups cake flour
2¼ teaspoons baking soda
½ teaspoon salt
1½ cups buttermilk
1 21-oz. can cherry pie filling
Cherries, fresh (optional)

Preheat oven to 350°.

In a large mixer bowl at medium speed, cream the shortening, sugar, and vanilla for several minutes or until smooth. Add egg whites and mix at medium speed for 5 minutes.

In a small bowl, combine water and cocoa; set aside.

In a medium bowl, combine flour, baking soda, and salt. Slowly add cocoa mixture and buttermilk to flour and blend well. Add creamed mixture slowly and continue to blend. Beat on low speed until mixture is smooth.

Spoon chocolate batter into paper-lined muffin tins, slightly over half full. Spoon cherry pie filling plus 2 or 3 fresh cherries (optional) in center of chocolate batter. Bake 25–30 minutes. Allow cupcakes to cool before removing them from pan. Makes 24–30 cupcakes.

Note: I do not frost these cupcakes but dust them with confectioner's sugar before serving.

PER SERVING (one cupcake):
Cholesterol (mg): 0
Fat (grams): total 9; saturated 3
Exchanges: milk 0; fruit 0; bread/starch 2;
vegetable 0; meat 0; fat 2
Calories: 250

Tangy Lemon Mousse

1 envelope unflavored gelatin
2 tablespoons cold water
¼ cup boiling water
2 egg whites, at room temperature
½ cup non-fat milk powder
½ cup water
¼ cup sugar
3 tablespoons lemon juice, freshly squeezed
1 teaspoon lemon rind, finely grated, divided
1 cup Mock Whipped Cream (optional) (pg. 238)

Soften gelatin in 2 tablespoons cold water for 3 minutes. Add boiling water and stir until gelatin is dissolved. Set aside.

Combine egg whites, non-fat milk powder, and ½ cup water in a large bowl. Beat with electric mixer until firm peaks form. Add dissolved gelatin and continue beating until thoroughly mixed.

Mix together, sugar, lemon juice, and ½ teaspoon lemon rind. Fold into the egg white mixture until color is even and no streaks of white show. Pour into 1½-qt. mold or individual 1-cup molds.

Refrigerate until firm. Before topping, sprinkle with remaining lemon rind or top with mock whipped cream and lemon rind. Makes 5 one-cup servings.

PER SERVING:
Cholesterol (mg): 2
Fat (grams): total 0; saturated 0
Exchanges: milk 1; fruit 0; bread/starch 0;
vegetable 0; meat 0; fat 0
Calories: 93

Cherry Cheesecake

½ cup graham cracker crumbs
3 tablespoons margarine, melted
2 8-oz. pkgs. plus 1 3-oz. pkg. Neufchatel
   cheese, softened
½ cup sugar
2 teaspoons lemon rind, grated
1 teaspoon vanilla
½ cup egg substitute
1 can cherry pie filling

Preheat oven to 350°.
Stir together, graham cracker crumbs and margarine. Press mixture evenly in bottom of a 9-in. springform pan. Bake 8 minutes. Cool.
Reduce oven temperature to 300°. Beat Neufchatel cheese in large mixer bowl. Add sugar, beating until fluffy. Add lemon rind and vanilla. Gradually add egg substitute, beating until well mixed. Pour over crumb shell.
Bake until center is firm, about 50 minutes. Cool in oven for 1 hour. Refrigerate until firm, 6 hours or overnight. Loosen edge of cheesecake by removing side of pan. Spread cherry pie filling over top and refrigerate until ready to serve. Serves 12.

PER SERVING:
Cholesterol (mg): 35
Fat (grams): total 14; saturated 7
Exchanges: milk 0; fruit 1; bread/starch 1;
vegetable 0; meat 0; fat 3
Calories: 252

Amaretto Cheesecake

CRUST
1 cup zwieback, finely crushed
2 tablespoons margarine, melted
1 tablespoon honey

FILLING

2 lbs. creamed low-fat cottage cheese

Egg substitute equal to 4 eggs

1 cup sugar

2 tablespoons flour

1 teaspoon vanilla

⅓ cup Amaretto

Crust: Combine zwieback crumbs, margarine, and honey. Mix well. Spread on bottom and sides of 10-in. springform pan.

Filling: In food processor or blender, combine all filling ingredients. Blend until smooth. Pour into crust. Bake in preheated 350° oven 45–60 minutes. Serves 12.

PER SERVING:

Cholesterol (mg): 3

Fat (grams): total 4; saturated 0

Exchanges: milk 0; fruit 0; bread/starch 2;

vegetable 0; meat 0; fat 1

Calories: 209

*

Apple Rice Pudding

2 cups rice, cooked

2 cups skim milk

1 cup apple pie filling

1 teaspoon vanilla

4 large egg whites

Salt, pinch

3 tablespoons sugar, or to taste

Cinnamon, ground

Low-fat yogurt (optional)

Preheat oven to 350°. Grease an 8-in. oven-proof casserole.

Combine rice, milk, apple pie filling, and vanilla in a medium bowl.

Put egg whites and salt in a mixing bowl. Slowly beat with mixer, adding sugar gradually, until soft peaks form.

Fold into rice mixture. Pour into casserole. Sprinkle with cinnamon.

Place casserole in a larger pan of water and bake 20 minutes. Remove casserole and stir. Return to oven and bake until set, about 20 minutes. Serve warm or at room temperature with a dollop of plain low-fat yogurt. Serves 4.

PER SERVING:
Cholesterol (mg): 5
Fat (grams): total 0; saturated 0
Exchanges: milk 0; fruit 2; bread/starch 2;
vegetable 0; meat 0; fat 0
Calories: 265

Irish Coffee Parfait

 2 envelopes unflavored gelatin
 ½ cup sugar
3½ cups boiling, strong-brewed coffee
 ¼ teaspoon cinammon
 ⅓ cup Irish whiskey
 1 cup Mock Whipped Cream (pg. 238)

Combine gelatin and sugar in a medium-size bowl. Stir in boiling coffee and cinnamon until sugar and gelatin dissolve. Stir in Irish whiskey.

Chill until gelatin is as thick as unbeaten egg whites. Pour mixture into 8 parfait glasses. Chill 2 hours or until gelatin is firm.

Prepare mock whipped cream and store in refrigerator until you are ready to serve the dessert. Before serving, spoon cream on top of coffee gelatin. Serve immediately. Serves 8.

PER SERVING:
Cholesterol (mg): 0
Fat (grams): total 0; saturated 0
Exchanges: milk 0; fruit 0; bread/starch 1;
vegetable 0; meat 0; fat 0
Calories: 92

Coeur à la Crème with Strawberries

1 cup low-fat cottage cheese
½ cup plain low-fat yogurt
2 tablespoons honey
½ teaspoon vanilla
2 cups fresh strawberries,* sliced
4 whole strawberries (for garnish)
4 teaspoons sugar; or 2 packets Equal
(optional)

Cut two squares of double-thick cheesecloth large enough to fit inside and over edges of four three-ounce *coeur à la crème* molds.** Wet the cheesecloth, wring well, and fit into the molds.

Put all ingredients except strawberries and sugar in blender and blend until smooth, turning off blender and scraping sides two or three times. Pour cheese mixture into molds. Place molds in a shallow dish to drain, 6 hours or overnight. After molds have drained, cover and refrigerate, 6 hours or overnight.

To serve, use edges of cheesecloth to pull cheese from molds. Invert onto a salad or dessert plate and remove cheesecloth. Spoon strawberries over cheese. Sprinkle with sugar or Equal if desired. Serves 4.

*Note: Raspberries, blueberries, or blackberries may also be used instead of strawberries.

**Note: If *coeur à la crème* molds are not available, a single mold can also be used.

PER SERVING:
Cholesterol (mg): 3
Fat (grams): total 0; saturated 0
Exchanges: milk 1; fruit 0; bread/starch 0;
vegetable 0; meat 0; fat 0
Calories: 87

Pavlova

3 large egg whites, at room temperature
3 tablespoons cold water
  Salt, pinch
1¼ cups sugar
  2 teaspoons cornstarch
  1 teaspoon white vinegar
  1 teaspoon vanilla
  1 cup Mock Whipped Cream (pg. 238)
1½ cups fresh-hulled strawberries, raspberries, blueberries, blackberries, or any combination of these

Preheat oven to 300°. Line cookie sheet with wax paper. Lightly grease both sides of paper with margarine. Outline a 7-in.-diam. circle on paper as a guide for size of the Pavlova.

Beat egg whites, water, and salt to soft peaks. Slowly beat in sugar and cornstarch. Continue beating until mixture holds stiff peaks, about 10 minutes. Add vinegar and vanilla while still beating. Beat until well mixed, about 2 minutes.

Lightly sprinkle wax paper with cold water. Using a spatula, scoop out mixture onto center of circle. Shape into 7-in. circle that is slightly mounded in center. Smooth top.

Bake in oven 30 minutes. Reduce heat to 250°. Continue to bake another 30 minutes. Remove to cooling rack. Cool 10 minutes. Carefully slide a long spatula under Pavlova to loosen it. Remove to flat surface and cool completely. Transfer Pavlova to serving platter, using 2 spatulas. Spoon the whipped topping into center. Decorate with berries. Serves 6.

PER SERVING:
Cholesterol (mg): 0
Fat (grams): total 0; saturated 0
Exchanges: milk 0; fruit 3; bread/starch 0;
vegetable 0; meat 0; fat 0
Calories: 186

Apple Flan

Pie pastry (pg. 239)
2 lbs. cooking apples
⅝ cup white wine (¼ pint)
½ lemon
4 tablespoons margarine
½ cup sugar
4 crisp eating apples
3 tablespoons apricot jam

Prepare pie pastry and roll it out on a lightly floured board into a thin round, large enough to line an 8-in.-diam. flan ring or shallow cake tin. Lift pastry on a rolling pin, line the flan ring, and trim off excess pastry.

Peel, core, and cut the cooking apples into quarters. Place them in a saucepan with the wine, strip of lemon rind (peel off with potato peeler), margarine, and ¼ cup of the sugar. Cover the pan and simmer gently until apples are very tender. Remove lemon rind.

Puree the apples in a food processor or by pressing through a sieve. Place the apple puree in the unbaked crust. Peel and core the eating apples, then slice thinly. Arrange the slices, overlapping, on top of the puree. Sprinkle with the remaining sugar and bake in moderately hot oven (375°) for 25–30 minutes.

Heat apricot jam in a small saucepan with 1 tablespoon lemon juice. Stir until well blended. Glaze the hot-cooked flan with apricot glaze. Serves 6.

PER SERVING:
Cholesterol (mg): 0
Fat (grams): total 7; saturated 10
Exchanges: milk 0; fruit 5; bread/starch 1;
vegetable 0; meat 0; fat 1
Calories: 425

✳

Devonshire Cream

½ cup fruit-only orange marmalade
¼ cup Curacao
2 tablespoons light brown sugar
2 tablespoons lemon juice
1 teaspoon lemon rind, grated
2 cups Mock Whipped Cream (pg. 238)

Combine marmalade, Curacao, brown sugar, lemon juice, and grated lemon rind in a small saucepan. Heat to boiling; stir until brown sugar is melted. Remove from heat and cool completely.

Beat mock whipped cream and ½ cup of the marmalade mixture in a large bowl with an electric mixer at high speed just until the cream mounds well and is thoroughly combined with the marmalade mixture. Spoon ½ cup of the mock whipped cream and marmalade mixture into a parfait or other tall crystal glass. Drizzle 1 tablespoon of remaining mixture over each before serving. Serves 8 (½-cup servings).

PER SERVING:
Cholesterol (mg): 0
Fat (grams): total 0; saturated 0
Exchanges: milk 0; fruit 0; bread/starch 1;
vegetable 0; meat 0; fat 0
Calories: 105

Mock Whipped Cream

1½ teaspoons unflavored gelatin
¼ cup boiling water
1½ teaspoons sugar
1 cup ice water
½ cup instant non-fat dry milk
2 teaspoons vanilla extract

Chill a large bowl and beaters. Dissolve gelatin in boiling water. Stir in sugar.

In chilled bowl, beat together ice water, non-fat dry milk, and vanilla until very frothy. Gradually add gelatin mixture and continue beating until quite stiff. Chill for at least 1 hour before using. Makes about 4 cups.

PER CUP:
Cholesterol (mg): 3
Fat (grams): total 0; saturated 0
Exchanges: milk 1; fruit 0; bread/starch 0;
vegetable 0; meat 0; fat 0
Calories: 66

Fresh Strawberry Rhubarb Pie

CRUST
1 recipe Nancy's Pastry (pg. 239)

FILLING
1 pt. fresh strawberries, washed and hulled
3 cups fresh rhubarb,* chopped
3 tablespoons honey
¼ cup cornstarch

Crust: Prepare pie crust. Preheat oven to 400° and place one pie crust in a 9-in. pan. Serves 8.

Filling: Combine all filling ingredients; mix lightly. Spoon into pie crust. Cut slits in several places. Bake at 400°

for 10 minutes. Lower temperature to 325° and bake 35 minutes more or until golden.

*Note: A 16-oz. package of frozen rhubarb may be substituted for the fresh rhubarb.

PER SERVING:
Cholesterol (mg): *0*
Fat (grams): *total 24; saturated 6*
Exchanges: *milk 0; fruit 1; bread/starch 1;*
vegetable 0; meat 0; fat 5
Calories: *375*

Nancy's Pastry for Pies and Tarts

      2 cups flour
1½ tablespoons salt
      1 cup Crisco
      ¼ cup ice water
      1 piece wax paper, 18-in. square

Combine flour and salt; cut in Crisco. Blend until mixture is the size of peas. Mix with about ¼ cup ice water. Blend well and divide into two balls. Wrap in wax paper and refrigerate 2 hours.

When you are ready to bake pie, remove pastry one ball at a time from refrigerator. Place square of wax paper on table and sprinkle with a little flour. Roll out pastry on waxed paper; this makes it easier to place pastry in pie pan because you can pick up rolled-out pie crust and invert it onto pan.

If you are making a two-crust pie, repeat with second ball of pastry and seal edges. If you are planning to use only one crust, crimp edges, using a fork.

PER SERVING:
Cholesterol (mg): *0*
Fat (grams): *total 194; saturated 51*
Calories: *2,496*

Breakfast

Having breakfast will help you stay on your low-cholesterol program because you will be less hungry during the day and better able to resist those temptations loaded with fat and cholesterol. I personally love breakfast and feel sorry for those people who have not discovered its pleasures and benefits. One of the reasons that I enjoy breakfast is because it provides a quiet time with my husband before the real work day begins and the phones start ringing. It gives us time to review the things we are going to do that day.

Before I eat breakfast, I have already exercised and completed the day's correspondence, so I have worked up a bit of an appetite. In fine weather, I enjoy one of my favorite things, breakfast on my patio. I can already hear you saying, I don't have time for that, I have to get the kids off to school, or it takes me an hour to get to work. Well, even if you can't enjoy breakfast during the week, make plans to savor it on the weekend. You might even catch up with a friend by inviting her or him to join you.

People argue about breakfast more than any other meal. They even argue about whether to have one at all. I believe that leaving out breakfast will undermine any diet. If you work in an office, take notice of the people eating Danish and doughnuts tomorrow morning with their coffee. Chance are, none of them have had breakfast.

Lack of time is no excuse to skip breakfast. For those who feel that they can't take time to eat before leaving for work, we have included recipes for breakfast treats that can be taken along. So no more excuses. As a matter of fact, if you take a batch of banana bran or apple raisin muffins or homemade bagels to work, you will listen to the raves. We have included in this chapter recipes for quick and easy breakfasts as well as those for more leisurely experiences.

Honey-Orange Spread

6 ozs. plain low-fat yogurt
4 teaspoons honey
1 teaspoon orange peel, grated

Whip together yogurt, honey, and orange peel with a fork until well blended and fluffy. Serve with muffins. Refrigerate leftovers. Makes 1 cup.

PER SERVING (one tablespoon):
Cholesterol (mg): 0
Fat (grams): total 0; saturated 0
Exchanges: milk 0; fruit 0; bread/starch 0;
vegetable 0; meat 0; fat 0
Calories: 11

Oat Muffins

2 cups oat flakes, divided
1¼ cups all-purpose flour
¼ cup firmly packed brown sugar
1 tablespoon baking powder
2 egg whites, slightly beaten
1 cup skim milk
3 tablespoons vegetable oil
¼ teaspoon cinnamon
½ cup golden raisins

Mix 1½ cups oat flakes with flour, brown sugar, and baking powder. Combine egg, milk, and oil; add to flour mixture and mix just enough to moisten flour. Add raisins and mix well.

Fill muffin pans sprayed with vegetable cooking spray about two-thirds full. Combine remaining cereal and cinnamon. Sprinkle over muffins. Bake at 400° for 15 minutes or until muffins spring back when lightly touched. Makes 12 muffins.

PER SERVING (one muffin):
Cholesterol (mg): 0
Fat (grams): total 4; saturated 0
Exchanges: milk 0; fruit 0; bread/starch 1;
vegetable 0; meat 0; fat 1
Calories: 135

Bran Muffins

¾ cup skim milk

½ cup unsweetened applesauce

1 egg

2 tablespoons vegetable oil

1 tablespoon honey

1 teaspoon orange peel, grated

1½ cups wheat bran cereal flakes

¾ cups all-purpose flour

½ cup whole-wheat flour

1 tablespoon baking powder

1 teaspoon ground cinnamon

½ cup dark raisins

¼ teaspoon nutmeg

Preheat oven to 400°. Spray muffin pan with vegetable cooking spray. Set aside.

In large bowl using a wire whisk, beat milk, applesauce, egg, oil, honey, and orange peel until thoroughly blended. Stir in bran cereal; let stand about 2 minutes to soften.

In a small bowl, combine flours, baking powder, cinnamon, raisins, and nutmeg; stir into bran mixture until just blended. Spoon batter into muffin cups. Bake 15–20 minutes or until golden. Serve warm. These muffins freeze well. Makes 12 muffins.

PER SERVING (one muffin):
Cholesterol (mg): 24
Fat (grams): total 3; saturated 0
Exchanges: milk 0; fruit 0; bread/starch 1;
vegetable 0; meat 0; fat 0
Calories: 109

Cherry Yogurt Cream Muffins

TOPPING
- 2 tablespoons sugar
- 2 tablespoons walnuts, finely chopped
- ¼ teaspoon cinnamon

MUFFINS
- 2 cups all-purpose flour
- ¾ cup sugar
- 2 teaspoons double-acting baking powder
- 1 teaspoon baking soda
- ¾ teaspoon salt
- 1 large whole egg plus 2 whites
- 1 cup low-fat yogurt
- 2 tablespoons skim milk
- ¾ stick (6 tablespoons) margarine, melted
- 1 teaspoon vanilla
- 1 cup (about ½ lb.) dried cherries, chopped

Topping: In a small bowl, combine sugar, walnuts, and cinnamon. Set aside.

Muffins: Sift flour, sugar, baking powder, baking soda, and salt into a large bowl. In another bowl, whisk together eggs, yogurt, milk, margarine, and vanilla. Make a well in the flour mixture, add the egg mixture, and stir with a wooden spoon until it is just blended. Stir in the cherries (batter will be lumpy).

Pour batter into 12 greased muffin tins, and sprinkle topping over the batter. Bake muffins in the middle of a preheated 400° oven for 15–20 minutes or until they are golden. Turn onto racks and let cool. Makes 12 muffins.

PER SERVING *(one muffin):*
Cholesterol (mg): *23*
Fat (grams): *total 7; saturated 1*
Exchanges: *milk 0; fruit 1; bread/starch 2; vegetable 0; meat 0; fat 1*
Calories: *242*

*

Carrot Raisin Muffins

2 cups all-purpose flour
¾ cup sugar
2 teaspoons double-acting baking powder
1 teaspoon baking soda
¾ teaspoon salt
1 large whole egg plus 2 whites
1 cup low-fat yogurt
2 tablespoons skim milk
¾ stick (6 tablespoons) margarine, melted
1 teaspoon vanilla
1½ cups carrots, grated
3 ozs. raisins

Sift flour, sugar, baking powder, baking soda, and salt into a large bowl. In another bowl, whisk together eggs, yogurt, milk, margarine, and vanilla. Make a well in the flour mixture, add the egg mixture, and stir with a wooden spoon until just blended. Stir in the carrots and raisins (batter will be lumpy).

Pour batter into 12 greased muffin cups. Bake muffins about 15 minutes in a preheated 400° oven. If they are not done, continue baking another 5 minutes or until golden. Turn onto racks and let cool. Makes 12 muffins.

PER SERVING (one muffin):
Cholesterol (mg): 23
Fat (grams): total 6; saturated 1
Exchanges: milk 0; fruit 0; bread/starch 2;
vegetable 0; meat 0; fat 1
Calories: 221

Banana Streusel Muffins

TOPPING

  2 tablespoons sugar

  2 tablespoons walnuts, finely chopped

  ¼ teaspoon cinnamon

MUFFINS

  2 cups all-purpose flour

  ¾ cup sugar

  2 teaspoons double-acting baking powder

  1 teaspoon baking soda

  ¾ teaspoon salt

  1 large whole egg plus 2 whites

  1 cup low-fat yogurt

  2 tablespoons skim milk

  ¾ stick (6 tablespoons) margarine, melted

  1 teaspoon vanilla

  3 large bananas (very ripe), mashed

Topping: In a small bowl, combine sugar, walnuts, and cinnamon. Set aside.

Muffins: Sift flour, sugar, baking powder, baking soda, and salt in a large bowl. In another bowl, whisk together eggs, yogurt, milk, margarine, and vanilla. Make a well in the flour mixture, add the egg mixture, and stir batter with a wooden spoon until blended. Stir in the bananas (batter will be lumpy).

Pour batter into 12 greased muffin tins and bake in the middle of a 400° oven 15–20 minutes. Turn onto racks and let cool. Makes 12 muffins.

PER SERVING (one muffin):
Cholesterol (mg): 23
Fat (grams): total 7; saturated 1
Exchanges: milk 0; fruit 0; bread/starch 2;
vegetable 0; meat 0; fat 1
Calories: 228

Lemon Yogurt Muffins with Poppy Seed

2 cups all-purpose flour
1 teaspoon baking powder
1 teaspoon baking soda
¼ cup sugar
2 tablespoons lemon juice
2 egg whites
1¼ cups plain low-fat yogurt
    Rind of 1 lemon, grated
2 tablespoons poppy seed
¼ cup (½ stick) margarine, melted

Preheat oven to 375° and spray muffin tins with vegetable cooking spray.

In a small mixing bowl, stir and toss together the flour, baking powder, and baking soda.

In another bowl, combine the sugar, lemon juice, egg whites, yogurt, lemon rind, poppy seed, and melted margarine. Mix well. Add the dry ingredients and beat until just blended.

Spoon batter into muffin tins, filling each about two-thirds full. Bake for about 15 minutes or until tops are lightly browned. Let them cool in the pan for a few minutes, then remove and serve warm. Makes 12 muffins.

PER SERVING (one muffin):
Cholesterol (mg): 0
Fat (grams): total 5; saturated 0
Exchanges: milk 0; fruit 0; bread/starch 1;
vegetable 0; meat 0; fat 1
Calories: 140

Banana Bran Muffins

1½ cups whole-wheat flour
1½ cups unprocessed bran
2 teaspoons baking soda
2 teaspoons cinnamon, ground
1 teaspoon nutmeg, ground
3 egg whites
½ cup honey
½ cup buttermilk
½ cup water
1 small ripe banana, mashed
1 teaspoon vanilla extract
Rind of 1 orange, grated

Preheat oven to 400°. Spray muffin tins with vegetable cooking spray.

In medium-size bowl, combine flour, bran, baking soda, cinnamon, and nutmeg.

In small bowl, mix egg whites, honey, buttermilk, water, banana, and vanilla. Add to flour mixture, stirring just until moistened. Add orange rind and mix well.

Pour batter into muffin tins, filling half full. Bake for 15 minutes or until wooden toothpick inserted in center comes out clean. Cool muffins in tins on wire rack. Remove from tins and serve immediately, or wrap and freeze until ready to use. Makes 24 muffins.

PER SERVING (one muffin):
Cholesterol (mg): 0
Fat (grams): total 0; saturated 0
Exchanges: milk 0; fruit 0; bread/starch 1;
vegetable 0; meat 0; fat 0
Calories: 63

✳
Apple Raisin Muffins

1 egg, beaten
¼ cup vegetable oil
½ cup sugar
1½ cups apples, peeled and finely chopped
2 cups all-purpose flour
1 tablespoon plus 1 teaspoon baking powder
½ teaspoon cinnamon
¼ teaspoon nutmeg
½ cup dark raisins
1 cup buttermilk
1 tablespoon sugar
½ teaspoon cinnamon

Combine egg, oil, and sugar. Mix well. In a medium bowl, combine apples, flour, baking powder, cinnamon, nutmeg, and raisins. Add to egg mixture along with buttermilk. Mix until just moistened.

Spray muffin tins with vegetable cooking spray. Pour batter into tins, filling two-thirds full.

Combine 1 tablespoon sugar and ½ teaspoon cinnamon and sprinkle over muffins. Bake at 374° for 20–25 minutes. Makes 15 muffins.

PER SERVING (one muffin):
Cholesterol (mg): 18
Fat (grams): total 4; saturated 0
Exchanges: milk 0; fruit 0; bread/starch 1;
vegetable 0; meat 0; fat 1
Calories: 145

Oatmeal Muffins

1 cup all-purpose flour
1 cup whole-wheat flour
1 cup quick-cooking oatmeal, uncooked
½ teaspoon cinnamon
¼ teaspoon nutmeg
3 teaspoons baking powder
1 cup apple juice
2 egg whites mixed with 1 yolk
¼ cup corn oil

In a bowl, mix flours, oatmeal, spices, and baking powder. Add apple juice, eggs, and oil; stir only until everything is moistened. Spray muffin pans with vegetable cooking spray and fill them about three-quarters full. Bake at 400° for 15–20 minutes or until puffed and golden brown. Serve warm. Makes 12 muffins.

PER SERVING (one muffin):
Cholesterol (mg): 23
Fat (grams): total 5; saturated 0
Exchanges: milk 0; fruit 0; bread/starch 1;
vegetable 0; meat 0; fat 1
Calories: 133

The Elegant Breakfast Muffin
This is a fast, nutritious breakfast that is also quite elegant

4 English muffins, split and toasted
1 cup fruit-only preserves, any flavor
8 ozs. low-fat cottage cheese or ricotta cheese
1 teaspoon vanilla
1 tablespoon margarine, melted
2 tablespoons brown sugar

Spread muffin halves equally with preserves, reserving 3 tablespoons. Blend cottage cheese with vanilla and spread over preserves on muffins. Drizzle each with melted margarine and sprinkle with brown sugar. Broil lightly until bubbly. Garnish with reserved preserves. Serves 4.

PER SERVING:
Cholesterol (mg): 2
Fat (grams): total 3; saturated 0
Exchanges: milk 0; fruit 2; bread/starch 4;
vegetable 0; meat 0; fat 0
Calories: 452

Egg-White Omelet with Cheese, Mushrooms, and Herbs

    1 teaspoon margarine
    6 egg whites
    2 ozs. low-cholesterol American cheese
    1 teaspoon fresh chives, minced
    ½ teaspoon fresh basil
    ¼ teaspoon thyme
    ½ teaspoon fresh parsley, minced
    2 tablespoons fresh mushrooms, sliced

Melt margarine in a small skillet over medium heat. Place egg whites, cheese, chives, basil, thyme, parsley, and mushrooms in the hot skillet. Cook 4–6 minutes until firm. Garnish with an orange slice if desired. Serves 2.

PER SERVING:
Cholesterol (mg): 3
Fat (grams): total 7; saturated 1
Exchanges: milk 0; fruit 0; bread/starch 0;
vegetable 0; meat 2; fat 1
Calories: 140

Mexican Omelet with Avocado Topping

2 tablespoons plain low-fat yogurt
1 tablespoon fresh cilantro (coriander), minced
1 teaspoon lemon juice
½ avocado, peeled and cut into small pieces
    Vegetable cooking spray
    Egg substitute equal to 4 eggs
¼ cup scallions, sliced
½ cup chunky-style bottled salsa, medium to
    hot, as desired

Put yogurt, cilantro, and lemon juice in a small bowl. Mix well. Add avocado and stir again.

Heat skillet on medium-high heat and spray with vegetable cooking spray. Add egg mixture and cook, stirring lightly, until mixture begins to set on bottom. Add onions and continue cooking until lightly set. Spoon salsa down the middle of the omelet. Loosen edges with spatula and fold in half. Carefully slide out of pan onto serving platter. Top with avocado mixture. Serves 2.

PER SERVING:
Cholesterol (mg): 0
Fat (grams): total 7; saturated 1
Exchanges: milk 0; fruit 0; bread/starch 1;
vegetable 1; meat 1; fat 1
Calories: 208

French Omelet

1 egg yolk
2 tablespoons vegetable oil
6 egg whites

2 tablespoons fresh herbs (rosemary, basil, thyme, and tarragon), finely chopped

Beat egg yolk with oil. Add egg whites and beat again until well blended. Brush an 8-in. skillet lightly with oil. Add half of the egg mixture to skillet. Cook, lifting edges to allow uncooked portion to run underneath. When omelet is lightly browned and firm, sprinkle with half of the herbs and roll up. Repeat with remaining egg mixture. Serves 2.

PER SERVING:
Cholesterol (mg): 136
Fat (grams): total 15; saturated 3
Exchanges: milk 0; fruit 0; bread/starch 0;
vegetable 0; meat 1; fat 3
Calories: 200

Cauliflower Omelet
This is an interesting brunch dish or a light supper

1 head cauliflower, about 1 lb., cut into 1½-in. slices
4 tablespoons margarine
1 tablespoon vegetable oil
1 large onion, finely chopped
8 egg whites and 1 yolk
1 tablespoon chives, minced
¼ cup fresh parsley, minced

In a large pot, steam cauliflower until done, about 20 minutes. Drain and reserve. Heat oven to 425°.

In a heavy frying pan with a heat-proof handle, melt margarine with oil. When hot, add onion. Cook and stir until onion is soft. Add reserved cauliflower and cook, turning occasionally, until onion and cauliflower are slightly browned. Arrange cauliflower in the skillet to make a single layer.

In a small bowl, whisk egg whites with the yolk until frothy. Pour over the cauliflower in the skillet. Gently shake pan to allow egg mixture to spread over cauliflower. Bake in the middle of the oven until omelet is firm, about 5 minutes. Invert onto a serving plate and sprinkle with chives and parsley. To serve, cut into wedges. Serves 4.

PER SERVING:
Cholesterol (mg): 68
Fat (grams): total 16; saturated 3
Exchanges: milk 0; fruit 0; bread/starch 0;
vegetable 0; meat 1; fat 3
Calories: 198

Renée's Eggless Challah Bread

1½ pkgs. dry yeast
1 tablespoon sugar
½ cup lukewarm water
4 cups all-purpose flour
1 cup lukewarm water
1 tablespoon sugar
1½ teaspoons salt
2 tablespoons homogenized shortening

Place yeast and 1 tablespoon sugar in a bowl. Add ½ cup lukewarm water, mixing well. The yeast should dissolve and start to bubble. Measure flour into a large bowl. Pour bubbling yeast into a well made in the center of the flour.

Add the remaining ingredients and knead the dough. Stand mixing bowl in a damp cloth to anchor it. Knead dough with the heel of your hand. Be sure to get all dough away from the sides and bottom of bowl. Keep kneading until dough begins to blister and comes off your hands. Lightly coat the surface of the dough with shortening. Cover bowl with a clean linen towel, and set it in a warm place to rise, about 40 minutes.

After rising, test dough by plunging your finger into center of the mound of dough. If your indentation remains, dough has risen sufficiently.

Divide dough into 4 parts. Pat and roll 3 of the parts into long cylinders; braid the 3 cylinders together. Divide the remaining part again into 3 small parts, form into cylinders, and braid. Place the small braid on top of the large braid.

Place dough on a greased baking sheet. Cover again with towel. Let rise in a warm place until dough is almost doubled, 30–40 minutes.

Place challah in a 400° oven and immediately reduce temperature to 375°; bake 50 minutes. The bread should be well browned and crusty. Cool on a rack. Serves 6.

Note: Brush surface of the loaf with an egg white and sprinkle with poppyseeds just before baking for a special crust.

PER SERVING:
Cholesterol (mg): 0
Fat (grams): total 4; saturated 1
Exchanges: milk 0; fruit 0; bread/starch 4;
vegetable 0; meat 0; fat 0
Calories: 321

Bagelmania
Homemade bagels without boiling!

4 tablespoons oil

2 tablespoons sugar

½ teaspoon salt

1 cup hot water

2 pkgs. dry yeast

1 egg

3¾ cups flour, sifted

Preheat oven to 400°.

Mix the oil, sugar, and salt with the hot water. When it cools to lukewarm, add yeast to dissolve.

Beat the egg until frothy. Add it to the liquid, then mix in the flour. Knead dough and shape it into a large ball; place in bowl and cover. When the dough has risen, knead it again and place it in the bowl, covered, to rise again. After the dough has risen for the second time, shape it into 12 doughnuts. Place on baking sheets and bake for 15 minutes at 400°. Lower the temperature to 350° and continue baking for 15 more minutes. Makes 12 bagels.

PER SERVING: (one bagel)
Cholesterol (mg): 23
Fat (grams): total 5; saturated 0
Exchanges: milk 0; fruit 0; bread/starch 2;
vegetable 0; meat 0; fat 1
Calories: 183

BIALYS

Prepare bagel dough as instructed above, but before baking, shape each into a ball and depress with a spoon. Saute 2 cups chopped onion until they are transparent. Fill each depression with onions and bake according to directions above.

Banana Bread

½ cup margarine, at room temperature
1 cup sugar
2 egg whites
1½ cups unbleached flour
1 teaspoon baking soda
1 cup very ripe bananas, mashed
½ cup low-fat yogurt
1 teaspoon vanilla
   Rind of 1 orange, grated

Preheat oven to 350°.

Cream margarine, sugar, and egg whites. Sift together dry ingredients and combine with margarine mixture. Add bananas, yogurt, and vanilla; stir well. Stir in orange rind, and pour into a 9x5x3-in. loaf pan (or 4 smaller pans) sprayed with vegetable cooking spray. Bake 1 hour (or about 40 minutes for smaller loaves). Turn out onto a rack to cool. Makes 1 large loaf or 4 small loaves. Large loaf has 4 servings.

PER SERVING:
Cholesterol (mg): 0
Fat (grams): total 6; saturated 1
Exchanges: milk 0; fruit ½; bread/starch 1;
vegetable 0; meat 0; fat 1
Calories: 162

Cranorange Bread

This is always part of my Christmas morn breakfast, and it makes a great gift also

2 cups whole-wheat flour
1½ teaspoons baking powder
½ teaspoon baking soda
1 tablespoon sugar
¾ cup frozen orange juice concentrate, thawed
¼ cup liquid egg substitute
2 tablespoons corn oil
2 teaspoons vanilla
1½ cups cranberries, blanched and coarsely chopped (1 cup chopped)
2 tablespoons fresh orange rind, grated

Preheat oven to 350°. Spray a 9x5-in. loaf pan with vegetable cooking spray.

Combine flour, baking powder, baking soda, and sugar in a large bowl and mix thoroughly. Combine orange juice concentrate, egg substitute, corn oil, and vanilla in another bowl and mix well.

Pour liquid ingredients into dry ingredients. Add cranberries and orange rind. Mix well and pour into sprayed loaf pan; bake until a wooden toothpick inserted comes out clean, 45–50 minutes. Makes 1 loaf, or 8 servings.

PER SERVING:
Cholesterol (mg): 0
Fat (grams): total 4; saturated 0
Exchanges: milk 0; fruit 1; bread/starch 1; vegetable 0; meat 0; fat 1
Calories: 178

✳
Swedish Pancakes

3 egg whites
1¾ cups skim milk, divided
6 tablespoons margarine, melted
1 cup cake flour
¼ teaspoon cinnamon
All-fruit preserves

Whisk egg whites in a large bowl. Add ¾ cup of milk to margarine and mix well. Add flour and cinnamon, and stir with a wooden spoon until smooth. Stir in remaining 1 cup of milk. Batter can be made in a blender or food processor if desired. Stir well and thin with milk as necessary. Result should be consistency of light cream.

Spray a large griddle with vegetable cooking spray and heat until very hot. Water droplets should dance on griddle when it is ready.

Pour batter, using 1 tablespoon for each pancake. Cook, turning once, until golden on both sides. It usually isn't necessary to add more cooking spray to griddle with subsequent batches, though you can do so if it seems necessary. Pancakes are usually served right away, but they can be kept warm in a 200° oven if you are making a large batch. Serve hot with preserves. Makes 18 pancakes.

Note: This batter can be made up to a day in advance if it is covered tightly.

PER PANCAKE:
Cholesterol (mg): 1
Fat (grams): total 5; saturated less than 1
Exchanges: milk 0; fruit 0; bread/starch ½;
vegetable 0; meat 0; fat 1
Calories: 70

Strawberry Cottage Cheese Crepes with Strawberry Sauce*

CREPES

    1 cup strawberries, hulled
    2 tablespoons sugar, divided
    1 cup cake flour
    ¾ cup cake flour
    ¾ cup low-fat cottage cheese
    3 egg whites and 1 yolk, lightly beaten
    1 teaspoon baking powder
    1½ teaspoons vanilla
    ⅛ teaspoon baking soda
    Salt, pinch
    Margarine, for cooking

STRAWBERRY SAUCE

    1½ cups strawberries, hulled and divided
    ⅔ cup honey

Crepes: Slice strawberries, toss with 1 tablespoon sugar, and put aside. Combine remaining ingredients, except margarine, and mix until just moistened. Mix in strawberries. Melt margarine in crepe pan and drop batter into pan by tablespoons. Cook until bubbles appear on top; then turn once. Crepes can be kept warm in a low oven while you finish cooking them and make the sauce.

Sauce: To make sauce, place 1 cup strawberries in blender with honey. Blend until berries are crushed, about 1 minute. Pour sauce over crepes and garnish with remaining strawberries. Makes about 24, 2½-in. crepes. Serves 6.

*Note: Not only is this a great brunch and breakfast recipe, but it is also a terrific dessert—very elegant.

PER SERVING:
Cholesterol (mg): 11
Fat (grams): total 0; saturated 0
Exchanges: milk 0; fruit 0; bread/starch 1;

vegetable 0; meat 0; fat 0
Calories: *70*

French Toast à l'Orange

Egg substitute equal to 4 eggs
4 tablespoons skim milk
½ cup orange juice
Rind of 1 orange, freshly grated
¼ teaspoon cinnamon
2 tablespoons margarine
4 slices whole-wheat bread
Maple syrup, light

In a wide bowl, whip egg substitute, milk, orange juice, rind, and cinnamon. Put skillet on stove over medium-high heat and add margarine. Dip bread in egg mixture to coat both sides and place in skillet. Cook until toast looks lightly browned on bottom when you lift it with a spatula, about 2 minutes. Turn toast over and brown other side. Serve with syrup. Makes 4 slices.

PER SERVING *(one slice):*
Cholesterol (mg): *0*
Fat (grams): *total 5; saturated 1*
Exchanges: *milk 0; fruit 0; bread/starch 1;*
vegetable 0; meat 1; fat 1
Calories: *181*

Baked French Toast with Peaches
This is best served in summer when peaches are at their best. Makes a great brunch dish

¼ cup dark brown sugar
¼ cup quick-cooking rolled oats
4 tablespoons margarine
½ cup golden raisins
½ teaspoon cinnamon
  Egg substitute equal to 2 eggs
8 slices whole-wheat bread
1 tablespoon sugar
4 medium-size ripe peaches, about 2 lbs.,
  thinly sliced
  Maple syrup, light (optional)
  Mock sour cream (optional)

Preheat oven to 375°.

Put brown sugar, oats, and margarine in small bowl. Cut in margarine until mixture resembles coarse crumbs. Stir in raisins and cinnamon. Reserve.

Lightly beat egg substitute in shallow dish. Dip bread slices on both sides into egg mixture, turning once to coat lightly. Allow excess to drip back into dish. Arrange bread on cookie sheet in single layer. Lightly sprinkle with sugar.

Arrange peach slices in rows to cover bread slices completely. Sprinkle reserved crumb topping over peaches. Bake until heated through and toast tops are lightly browned, 10–12 minutes. Remove from oven. Arrange on individual serving plates and garnish with strawberries. Both maple syrup and mock sour cream go well with this toast. Makes 8 slices.

PER SERVING (one slice):
Cholesterol (mg): 0
Fat (grams): total 5; saturated 1
Exchanges: milk 0; fruit ½; bread/starch 2; vegetable 0; meat 0; fat 1
Calories: 225

Beverages

Beverages can be more interesting than a cup of coffee or a glass of lemonade. A cool beverage can quench your thirst on a hot summer's day or warm a skier after an afternoon in the snow. And a low-cholesterol eating program can benefit from creative beverages that are not laden with sugar and fats, as are most regular soft-drinks, milkshakes, and hard liquor.

You can combine fruit flavors, spices, or liqueurs to create beverages for any special occasion. Here, you will find tasty fruit punches, warm comforting drinks, and light aperitifs that can be enjoyed by themselves or with meals.

Whatever the occasion, be it a wedding, quick lunch, picnic, or cocktail party, you'll find just the right recipe in this chapter.

✳

Russian Tea

  2 tablespoons whole cloves
  8 cups water
 10 tea bags
  ½ cup sugar
  2 cups orange juice
  2 cups peach juice
    Juice of 1 lemon

Boil cloves in water for 3 minutes. Add tea bags; let steep for 5 minutes. Strain. Add sugar and juices; reheat. Serve hot. Serves 24.

PER SERVING:
Cholesterol (mg): 0
Fat (grams): total 0; saturated 0
Exchanges: milk 0; fruit ½; bread/starch 0;
vegetable 0; meat 0; fat 0
Calories: 25

✳

Café Brulot

  2 ozs. brandy
  2 sugar cubes
  2 cinnamon sticks
  2 whole cloves
  1 curl of lemon peel
  1 curl of orange peel
  2 cups hot coffee, freshly made

Combine all ingredients except coffee in silver bowl. Flame. Ladle until sugar has dissolved; add coffee. Serve in demitasse cups. Serves 4.

PER SERVING:
Cholesterol (mg): 0
Fat (grams): total 0; saturated 0

Exchanges: milk 0; fruit ½; bread/starch 0;
vegetable 0; meat 0; fat 1
Calories: 62

Iced Mocha Coffee

2 ozs. sweet cooking chocolate
1⅓ cups skim milk
¼ cup sugar
1½ teaspoons cinnamon, ground
2 teaspoons vanilla extract
3 cups hot, double-strength coffee
½ teaspoon mocha extract
⅓ cup non-dairy topping

Break chocolate into pieces. Melt it with milk, sugar, and cinnamon in top of a double boiler over gently simmering water. Stir chocolate mixture and vanilla into coffee. Refrigerate until well chilled or overnight. Remove from refrigerator and add mocha extract; stir well. To serve, add ice cubes to tall, frosted glasses and fill with coffee. Top with a dollop of topping, stirring topping lightly so it covers top of glass. Serve immediately. Serves 4.

PER SERVING:
Cholesterol (mg): 1
Fat (grams): total 8; saturated 5
Exchanges: milk 0; fruit 0; bread/starch 1;
vegetable 0; meat 0; fat 2
Calories: 163

✳

Mocha Java

1½ cups strong, hot coffee
   4 tablespoons Tia Maria Liqueur
   2 teaspoons sugar
   ½ teaspoon cinnamon
Garnish:
1½ teaspoons Tia Maria Liqueur
   ½ teaspoon sugar
   4 tablespoons non-dairy topping

Stir ½ of the coffee, Tia Maria, sugar, and cinnamon together in a mug.

For garnish, fold Tia Maria and sugar into topping. Divide between both mugs and drizzle over the coffee. Serves 2.

PER SERVING:
Cholesterol (mg): 0
Fat (grams): total 2; saturated 2
Exchanges: milk 0; fruit 2; bread/starch 0;
vegetable 0; meat 0; fat 1
Calories: 153

✳

Carrot Mary

1 12-oz. can carrot juice, chilled
1 18-oz. can tomato juice, chilled
½ teaspoon celery seeds
⅛ teaspoon hot pepper sauce
1 teaspoon horseradish
½ teaspoon cracked pepper
   Carrot sticks
   Parsley sprigs

Combine juices in pitcher. Add celery seeds, hot pepper sauce, horseradish, and cracked pepper. Serve in tall, frosted glasses over ice cubes, garnished with carrot sticks and parsley sprigs. Serves 4.

PER SERVING:
Cholesterol (mg): 0
Fat (grams): total 0; saturated 0
Exchanges: milk 0; fruit 0; bread/starch 0;
vegetable 3; meat 0; fat 0
Calories: 69

Cider Punch

   Grated rind of ½ lemon
 1 qt. apple cider
 1 cup dry red wine
 ½ cup superfine sugar
   Juice of 1 lemon
 1 tablespoon orange rind, grated
 ½ cup brandy
 1 orange, sliced thin

In a punch bowl, combine lemon rind, cider, and red wine. Let stand for 30 minutes. Add sugar, lemon juice, and orange rind. Stir to dissolve sugar. Chill in refrigerator until serving time. Just before serving, stir in brandy and float orange slices on top of punch. Serves 6–8.

PER SERVING:
Cholesterol (mg): 0
Fat (grams): total 0; saturated 0
Exchanges: milk 0; fruit 2; bread/starch 0;
vegetable 0; meat 0; fat 1
Calories: 183

✳
Apple Cider Medley

1½ cups apple cider
  2 tablespoons diet maple syrup or low-cal
    syrup
  2 tablespoons Cointreau
  2 tablespoons brandy
  2 teaspoons margarine, softened
    Nutmeg, freshly grated
  1 cinnamon stick

Bring cider and syrup to a boil. Pour into a mug and stir in Cointreau, brandy, and margarine. Grate nutmeg over top and serve immediately with a cinnamon stick. Serves 2.

PER SERVING:
Cholesterol (mg): 0
Fat (grams): total 6; saturated 1
Exchanges: milk 0; fruit 2; bread/starch 0;
vegetable 0; meat 0; fat 3
Calories: 235

✳
Precious Peach Punch

  3 fresh peaches, peeled and sliced
  1 cinnamon stick
  1 bottle (750 ml) peach wine*
  1 bottle (750 ml) champagne
  ¼ cup lemon juice

Put peaches into 2-qt. punch bowl. Break cinnamon stick into pieces; add to peaches. Pour in peach wine. Cover and chill overnight. Strain wine and add champagne and lemon juice just before serving. Garnish each glass with a single slice of peach. Makes 12 one-half cup servings.

  *Note: Source of dessert wine: Galena Cellars, 515 S. Main st., Galena, Il. Castel Loris distributed by Hunter Bros. Wine Distributing, Inc., Cleveland, OH 44115

PER SERVING:
Cholesterol (mg): 0
Fat (grams): total 0; saturated 0
Exchanges: milk 0; fruit 1; bread/starch 0;
vegetable 0; meat 0; fat 2
Calories: 137

Cranberry Punch

3 pts. cranberry juice cocktail
2 cups orange juice
2 tablespoons lemon juice
2 cups sugar
3 cinnamon sticks
1 teaspoon cloves

Combine all ingredients in saucepan; bring to a boil. Simmer for 1–2 minutes. Dilute with 2 qts. water; chill. Serves 16.

PER SERVING:
Cholesterol (mg): 0
Fat (grams): total 0; saturated 0
Exchanges: milk 0; fruit 3; bread/starch 0;
vegetable 0; meat 0; fat
Calories: 160

✳
Sangria Slush

3 cups fresh pineapple, chopped
2 cups orange sections (about 6 oranges)
2 cups sliced peaches (about 6 small peaches)
6 tablespoons frozen lemonade concentrate,
    thawed
2½ cups dry red wine, chilled and divided
1 cup club soda, chilled
1 lemon, sliced thin
1 orange, sliced thin
1 peach, sliced thin
8 fresh pineapple chunks

Arrange chopped pineapple, orange sections, and peaches in a single layer on a baking sheet; freeze until firm.

In blender or food processor, add fruit and process until chunky. Add lemonade concentrate and 1½ cups wine; process until smooth. Pour into a large pitcher; add remaining 1 cup wine and club soda. Stir well.

Float lemon, orange, peach, and pineapple chunks in pitcher. Pour Sangria into individual glasses and garnish with fruit slices. Makes about 2 quarts, or 8 one-cup servings.

PER SERVING:
Cholesterol (mg): 0
Fat (grams): total 0; saturated 0
Exchanges: milk 0; fruit 2; bread/starch 0;
vegetable 0; meat 0; fat 1
Calories: 168

✳
Italian Mulled Wine

> **2 qts. dry red wine**
> **8 thin lemon slices**
> **8 thin orange slices**
> **6 tablespoons sugar**
> **4–6 sticks cinnamon**
> **1 pear, sliced thin**
> **6 whole cloves**

Place all ingredients in large kettle over low heat; bring to boiling point. Ignite and allow to burn for 1 minute. Strain if desired, and serve hot. Serves 8.

PER SERVING:
Cholesterol (mg): 0
Fat (grams): total 0; saturated 0
Exchanges: milk 0; fruit 1; bread/starch 0;
vegetable 0; meat 0; fat 3
Calories: 217

Brand Index

Bisquick: General Mills, Inc., Minneapolis, MN 55440.

Coffee Rich: Non-dairy creamer made with soybean oil that is 100 percent cholesterol free and low in saturated fat.

Egg Beaters: Nabisco Brands, Inc., East Hanover, NJ 07936.

Hellman's Light Mayonnaise: Best Foods International, Inc., Englewood Cliffs, NJ 07632.

I Can't Believe It's Not Butter: Margarine. Lever Brothers Co., New York, NY 10022.

Seastix Imitation Crab Meat: Kibun Products International, Raleigh, NC 27629.

Sorrell Ridge Fruit Only Conserve: Sorrel Ridge Farm, 100 Markley St., Port Reading, NJ 07064.

Spike: A blend of 39 spices. Gaylord Hauser, distributed by Modern Products, Inc., P.O. Box 093209, Milwaukee, WI 53209.

Tamari Soy Sauce: Arrowheat Mills, Inc., Hereford, TX 79045.

Index

A

Acorn Squash, 195
Amaretto Cheesecake, 231
Antipasto Salad, 96
Appetizers, 24–40
  Artichoke Dip, 26
  Caponata, 40
  Celery, stuffed, 25
  Eggs, Deviled, 39
  Hummus, 27
  Italian Bruschetta, 26
  Melon Balls in Lambrusco, 37
  Mushrooms and Artichoke
    Hearts, marinated, 35
  Mushroom Caps, Salmon-
    filled, 38
  Mushrooms, Cheese-stuffed, 31
  Mushroom Paté, 28
  Quiche, 29
  Scallops in Mustard-Dill
    Sauce, 30
  Tabouleh, 33
  Tart, Onion, 34
  Tomatoes, baked and
    stuffed, 36
  Tomatoes with Mozzarella, 38
  Vegetable Caviar, 32
Apple Cider Medley, 268
Apple Flan, 236
Apple Raisin Muffins, 249
Apple Rice Pudding, 232
Arroz con Tomate (Spanish
  Rice), 173
Artichoke Dip, 26
Asparagus with Mustard
  Cream, 205
Asparagus Pie, 183
Asparagus Salad Supreme, 92
Asparagus, Stir-Fried, 200
Asparagus Vinaigrette, 69

B

Bagels, 256
Banana Bran Muffins, 248
Banana Bread, 257
Banana Dressing, 97
Banana Streusel Muffins, 246
Basque Vegetable Soup, 48
Bean Soup, Italian, 57
Bean, South-of-the-Border,
  Salad, 91
Bean Stew, 184
Beef, 108–17
Beef Broth, 42
Beef Burgundy, 111
Beef and Mushroom Stir-Fry, 110
Beef Stew, 114
Beef Stroganoff, 109
Beets Mandarin, 80
Beverages, 263–71
Bialy, 256
Blueberry Bavarian Salad, 71
Boeuf à la Bourguignon, 111
Bouillabaisse, 151
Bran Muffins, 243, 248
Bread, 254–59
  Banana, 257
  Challah, 254
  Cranorange, 258
  Swedish, 259
Breakfast, 240–262
Broccoli, Basque, 54
Broccoli Casserole, 208
Broccoli Salad, 76
Broth, Beef, 42
Brownies, 228
Brown Rice and Chicken Salad, 83
Bruschetta, Italian, 26
Burgers, Salmon, 145
Burgers, Turkey, 118
Burgers, Vegetable, 182

For more healthful meals, at home and in restaurants,
consider these titles from Surrey Books . . .

(please turn the page)